Guitar Chord Songbook

Beach Boys

ISBN 0-634-05617-4

HAL•LEONARD®
CORPORATION

7777 W. BLUEMOUND RD. P.O. BOX 13819 MILWAUKEE, WI 53213

For all works contained herein:
Unauthorized copying, arranging, adapting, recording or public performance is an infringement of copyright.
Infringers are liable under the law.

Visit Hal Leonard Online at
www.halleonard.com

Contents

4   Add Some Music to Your Day

10   All Summer Long

12   Barbara Ann

7   Be True to Your School

14   Cabinessence

20   California Girls

22   Caroline, No

24   Catch a Wave

26   Cherry Cherry Coupe

17   Cotton Fields (The Cotton Song)

28   Country Air

30   Custom Machine

32   Dance, Dance, Dance

35   Darlin'

38   Do It Again

40   Do You Remember?

42   Don't Back Down

44   Don't Talk

46   Don't Worry Baby

48   Drive In

50   409

52   Friends

55   Fun, Fun, Fun

58   Girl Don't Tell Me

60   Girls on the Beach

62   God Only Knows

64   Good Vibrations

70   Hawaii

67	Help Me Rhonda
72	Here Today
75	Heroes and Villains
78	I Get Around
81	I Just Wasn't Made for These Times
84	In My Room
86	It's OK
88	Keep an Eye on Summer
90	Kokomo
94	Let Him Run Wild
96	Little Deuce Coupe
98	The Little Girl I Once Knew
102	Little Honda
104	Little Saint Nick
106	Please Let Me Wonder
101	Salt Lake City
108	Shut Down
110	Sloop John B
113	Spirit of America
116	Surf's Up
120	Surfer's Rule
122	Surfin' U.S.A.
124	That's Not Me
126	The Warmth of the Sun
128	Wendy
131	When I Grow Up (To Be a Man)
142	Wild Honey
134	Wind Chimes
136	Wouldn't It Be Nice
138	You Still Believe in Me
140	You're So Good to Me

Add Some Music to Your Day

Words and Music by Brian Wilson,
Mike Love and J. Knott

Melody:

The Sun-day morn-ing gos - pel goes good with the sun. _

(Capo 2nd fret)

| D | G | C | A | Bm | F#m |
| B7 | Em | F#7 | E7 | Dmaj7 | Gmaj7 |

Intro | D | | |

Verse 1

        D
The Sunday morning gospel

Goes good with the sun.
       G
There's Blues, Folk and Country
               D
And Rock like a rollin' stone.
    C   **D**
The world could come together as one
    C   **D**
If ev'rybody under the sun
          G   **A**   **D**
Adds some music   to your day.

Copyright © 1970 (Renewed 1998) Brother Publishing Company (BMI)
All Rights Reserved   Used by Permission

Verse 2

D
You'll hear it while your walkin'

By a neighbor's home.
G
You'll hear it faintly in the distance
                          D
When you're on the phone.
   C   **D**
You're sittin' in a dentist's chair,
   C   **D**
And they got music for you there,
            G   **A**   **D**
To add some music   to your day.

Chorus

D
Add some music.

Add some music.
G
Add some, add some,

Add some, add some
D
Music.
    C   **D**
Your doctor knows it keeps you calm.
    C   **D**
Your preacher adds it to his psalms.
         G   **A**   **D**
So add some music   to your day.

Bridge

Bm   F#m
Music, when you're alone

               B7
Is like a com-panion

                   Em
For your's only soul.

     F#7
Oh,

       B7
Whoa,

       E7
Whoa,

    A
Oh, ___ oo.

Interlude

Dmaj7   Gmaj7
   When day is over,
Dmaj7   Gmaj7
   I close my tired eyes.
Bm   A   Bm   A
Music is in my soul.

Verse 3

               D
At a movie you can feel it

 Touching your heart.
          G
And on ev'ry day of the summertime
            D
You'll hear children chasing ice-cream cars.
        C   D
They'll play it on your wedding day;
        C   D
There must be 'bout a million ways
            G   A   D
To add some music   to your day.

Outro

       D
‖: Add some music to your day.

Add some music to your day. :‖ *Repeat and fade*

Be True to Your School

Words and Music by
Brian Wilson and Mike Love

When some loud brag-gart tries to put me down, __

(Capo 3rd fret)

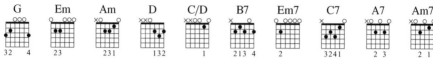

                 G
Intro   When some loud braggart

                       Em
           Tries to put me down,

                       Am
           And says his school is great,

           D
            I tell him right away,

                 G
           "Now, what's the matter, buddy,

                    Em
           Ain't you heard of my school?

                    Am   **D**   **C/D**   **D**
           It's number one in the state."

                 C/D   **G**
Chorus 1   So be __ true to your school __ now,

                           B7
           Just like you would to your girl ____ or guy.

                     Em7
           Be true to your school ____ now

                    C7
           And let your colors fly.

     A7   **Am7** **D** **C/D** **D** **C/D**
            Be true to your school.

Copyright © 1963 IRVING MUSIC, INC.
Copyright Renewed
All Rights Reserved   Used by Permission

Verse 1

        G
I got a letterman sweater

        Em7
With the letter in front

        Am7
I got for football and track.

        D
I'm proud to wear it.

        G
Now, when I cruise around

        Em7
The other parts of the town,

        Am7
I got a decal in back.

Chorus 2

      D   **G**
So be true to your school __ now,

                 B7
Just like you would to your girl __ or guy.

           Em7
Be true to your school ____ now

           C7
And let your colors fly.

A7   **Am7**
  Be true to your school.

| **D** | **C/D** | **D** | **C/D** | |

Verse 2

       G
Come Friday, we'll be jacked up

      Em7
On the football game,

       Am7
And I'll be ready to fight.

       D
We're gonna smash 'em now.

     G
My girly will be working

     Em7
On her pompoms now,

      Am7
And she'll be yelling tonight.

Chorus 3

      D   **G**
So be true to your school __ now,

               B7
Just like you would to your girl __ or guy.

         Em7
Be true to your school __ now,

        C7
And let your colors fly.

A7   **Am7**
  Be true to your school.

| D   C/D | D   C/D |

Outro

     G   **Em7**
‖: Ra, ra, ra, be true to your school.

Am7   **D**
Ra, ra, ra, be true to your school. :‖ *Repeat and fade*

All Summer Long

Words and Music by
Brian Wilson and Mike Love

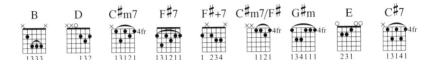

B D C♯m7 F♯7 F♯+7 C♯m7/F♯ G♯m E C♯7

Verse 1

      B   **D**
Sittin' in my car outside your house,

  C♯m7   **F♯7 F♯+7**
  'Member when you spilled Coke all over your blouse?

  B   **D**
Tee shirts, cut offs, and a pair of thongs.

  C♯m7   **C♯m7/F♯**   **G♯m** **B**
  We've been havin' fun ____ all summer long.

Chorus

                E
All summer long you've been with me;

   B
I can't see enough of you.

               E
All summer long we've both been free;

  C♯7   **F♯7**   **F♯+7**
Won't be long till summertime is through.

Copyright © 1964 IRVING MUSIC, INC.
Copyright Renewed
All Rights Reserved   Used by Permission

Verse 2

B   D
Miniature golf and Hondas in the hills;

C♯m7   F♯7 F♯+7
  When we rode that horse we got some thrills.

B   D
Ev'ry now and then we hear our songs.

C♯m7   C♯m7/F♯   G♯m   B
  We've been havin' fun ___ all summer long.

Interlude

| E | | B | |

| E | |

C♯7   F♯7 F♯+7
Won't be long till summertime is through.

Outro

B   D
Ev'ry now and then we hear our songs.

C♯m7   C♯m7/F♯   B   C♯m7
  We've been havin' fun ___ all summer long.

   B   D
‖: We've been havin' fun all summer long.   :‖ *Repeat and fade*

Barbara Ann

Words and Music by Fred Fassert

Melody:

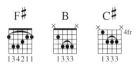

Ba, ba, ba, ba, ___ Ba - b'ra Ann.

F#   B   C#

134211   1333   1333

Chorus 1

N.C.
(Ba, ba, ba, ba, Ba'bra Ann.

Ba, ba, ba, ba, Ba'bra Ann.)

F#   B
Ba'bra Ann, take my hand.

F#   C#
Ba'bra Ann, you got me rockin' and a rollin',

B   F#
Rock - in' and a reelin', Ba'bra Ann,

Ba, ba, ba, Ba'bra Ann.

Verse 1

F#
Went to a dance, lookin' for romance,

Saw Ba'bra Ann, so I thought I'd take a chance.

B
Oh, Ba'bra Ann, Ba'bra Ann, take my hand.

F#
Oh, Ba'bra Ann, Ba'bra Ann, take my hand.

C#
You got me rockin' and a rollin',

B   F#
Rock - in' and a reelin', Ba'bra Ann,

Ba, ba, ba, Ba'bra Ann.

© 1959 (Renewed 1987) EMI LONGITUDE MUSIC and COUSINS MUSIC INC.
All Rights Controlled and Administered by EMI LONGITUDE MUSIC
All Rights Reserved   International Copyright Secured   Used by Permission

Chorus 2   *Repeat Chorus 1*

Verse 2
F#
Played my fav'rite tune, danced with Betty Lou,

Tried Peggy Sue, but I knew they wouldn't do.
      B
Oh, Ba'bra Ann, Ba'bra Ann, take my hand.
      F#
Oh, Ba'bra Ann, Ba'bra Ann, take my hand.
     C#
You got me rockin' and a rollin',
     B   F#
Rock - in' and a reelin', Ba'bra Ann,

Ba, ba, ba, Ba'bra Ann.

Chorus 3   *Repeat Chorus 1*

Cabinessence

Words and Music by
Brian Wilson and Van Dyke Parks

Melody:

Light the lamp and ___ fi - re mel-low;

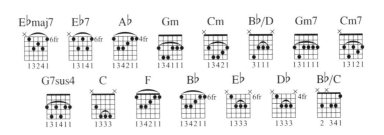

Verse 1

Eᵇmaj7　　　　　　Eᵇ7
Light the lamp and ____ fire mellow;

Aᵇ　　　　Gm　　　Cm
Cabinessence ____ timely hello

Bᵇ/D　　　　Gm7　　Cm7
Welcomes the time for a change.

Eᵇmaj7　　　　　　　Eᵇ7
Lost and found, you ____ still remain there.

Aᵇ　　　　　　Gm　　　　　Cm
You'll find a meadow ____ filled with grain there.

Bᵇ/D　　　　G7sus4　　C
I'll give you a home on the range.

Copyright © 1968 IRVING MUSIC, INC.
Copyright Renewed
All Rights Reserved   Used by Permission

	F
Chorus 1	Who ran the iron horse?

Who ran the iron horse?

Who ran the iron horse?

Who ran the iron horse?
B♭
Who ran the iron horse?

Who ran the iron horse?

Who ran the iron horse?

Who ran the iron horse?
F
Who ran the iron horse?

Who ran the iron horse?

	E♭maj7 E♭7
Verse 2	I want to watch you ____ windblown facing

A♭   **Gm**   **Cm**
Waves of wheat for ____ your em-bracing.

B♭/D   **Gm7**   **Cm7**
Folks sing a song of the grange.

E♭maj7   **E♭7**
Nestle in a ____ kiss below there.

A♭   **Gm**   **Cm**
The constellations ____ ebb and flow there

B♭/D   **G7sus4**   **C**
And witness our home on the range.

Chorus 2   *Repeat Chorus 1*

                              Cm   **E♭**

Outro   Have you seen the grand coolie

                   F   **A♭**

Workin' on the railroad?

B♭   **D♭**

Have you seen the grand coolie

E♭

Workin' on the railroad?

  B♭/C

‖: Over and over,

The crow cries uncover the cornfield.

Over and over,

The thresher and hover the wheat field. :‖ ***Repeat and fade***

Cotton Fields
(The Cotton Song)

Words and Music by Huddie Ledbetter

Melody:

When I was a lit - tle bit - ty ba - by

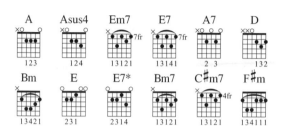

Chorus 1

   A
When I was a little bitty baby

My mama done rocked me in the cradle,

         Asus4 A   **Em7 E7   Em7 E7**
In them old   cotton fields back home.

     A   **A7**
It was back in Louisian - a,

      D   **A**
Just about a mile from Texar-kana

      Bm   **E**   **A**
In them old cotton fields __ back home.

TRO - © Copyright 1962 (Renewed) Folkways Music Publishers, Inc., New York, NY
International Copyright Secured
All Rights Reserved Including Public Performance For Profit
Used by Permission

Verse 1

A

Let me tell you now, well, I got me in a fix.

I caught a nail in my tire doin' licketey-splits.

                                                  E7*

I had to walk a long, long way to town.

             A

Came along a nice old man with a,

A7

  He had a hat on.

D

Wait a minute, mister,

      Bm7

Can you give me some direction?

A   Bm   E   A

  I'm gonna want to be right off for __ home.

Chorus 2

           A

When I was a little bitty baby

My mama done rocked me in the cradle,

                      E7*

In them old cotton fields back home.

      A   A7

It was back in Louisian - a,

            D   Bm7

Just about a mile from Texarkan - a

          A Bm   E   A

In them old __ cotton fields __ back home.

Bridge

                D

Don't care if them cotton balls get rotten.

           A

When I got you, __ baby, who needs cotton.

                   Bm7   E7*

In them old cotton fields back home.

Verse 2
```
                        A
Brother, only one thing more that's
A7
    Gonna warm ya,
D                         Bm7
    A summer's day out in California.
A                    Bm        E        A
    It's gonna be them cotton fields __ back __ home.
```

Interlude
```
| Bm7 C♯m7 D    E   | Bm7    E    A |                   |
```

Outro
```
          D
It was back in Louisiana
              A                 F♯m
Just about a mile from Texarkan  -  a
                    A
That give me them cotton fields.
F♯m                  A          F♯m
    Let me hear it for the cotton fields.
A                    F♯m           Bm7        E7*
    You know that there's just no place like home.
          A
Well, boy, it sure feels good
          A7
To breath the air back home;
              D
You should've seen their faces
          Bm7
When they seen how I'd grown.
          A Bm      E     D     A
In them old cotton fields __ back home.
‖: A          |              :‖ Repeat and fade
```

California Girls

Words and Music by
Brian Wilson and Mike Love

Melody:

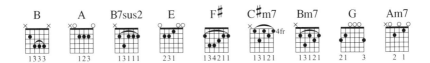

Well, East Coast girls are hip, ___ I

B   A   B7sus2   E   F#   C#m7   Bm7   G   Am7

Intro   ‖: B | :‖ *Play 4 times*

| A | | B | |

Verse 1

       B
Well, East Coast girls are hip,

       B7sus2
I really dig ___ those styles they wear.

       E
And the Southern girls with the way they talk,

       F#
They knock me out when I'm down there.

       B
The Midwest farmer's daughters

       B7sus2
Really make you feel alright.

       E
And the Northern girls with the way they kiss,

       F#
They keep their boyfriends warm at night.

Copyright © 1965 IRVING MUSIC, INC.
Copyright Renewed
All Rights Reserved   Used by Permission

Chorus 1

      B   C#m7
I wish they all could be ___ California

       A   Bm7
girls.
    (I wish they all could be ___ California...)
   G   Am7   B
I wish they all could be ___ California girls.

Verse 2

   B
The West Coast has the sunshine,

     B7sus2
And the girls all get so tan.

     E
I dig a French bikini on Hawaiian island dolls

    F#
By a palm tree in the sand.

   B
I've been all around this great big world

     B7sus2
And I see all kinds of girls.

      E
Yeah, but I couldn't wait to get back in the States,

      F#
Back to the cutest girls in the world.

Chorus 2   *Repeat Chorus 1*

Interlude | B | C#m7 |

Outro

     B
‖: I wish they all could be California

    C#m7
girls.
   I wish they all could be California girls. :‖ ***Repeat and fade***

Caroline, No

Words and Music by
Brian Wilson and Tony Asher

Melody:

Where did   your long hair   go?

(Capo 6th fret)

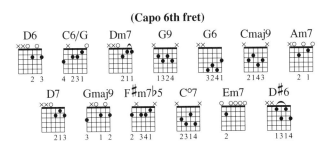

D6   C6/G   Dm7   G9   G6   Cmaj9   Am7

D7   Gmaj9   F#m7♭5   C°7   Em7   D#6

Verse 1

| **D6** | **C6/G** |
Where did your long hair go?

| **D6** | **C6/G** |
Where is the girl I used to know?

| **D6** | **Dm7** | **G9** | **G6** |
How could you lose that happy glow?

Cmaj9
Oh, Caroline, ____ no.

Verse 2

D6   **C6/G**
Who took that look away?

D6   **C6/G**
I remember how you used to say

D6   **Dm7** **G9**   **G6**
You'd never change, ___ but that's not true.

Copyright © 1966 IRVING MUSIC, INC.
Copyright Renewed
All Rights Reserved   Used by Permission

Bridge

           Cmaj9   **Am7**
Oh, Caroline, ___ you break my heart.

   D7   **Gmaj9**
I really want to go and cry.

    F♯m7♭5   **C°7**   **Em7**
It's so ___ sad to watch a sweet thing die.

           D♯6
Oh, Caroline, ___ why?

Verse 3

D6   **C6/G**
  Could I ever find in you again

D6   **C6/G**
  Things that made me love you so much then?

D6   **Dm7**   **G9**   **G6**
  Could we ever bring 'em back once they have gone?

         Cmaj9
Oh, Caroline, ___ no.

Outro

‖: **D6** | **C6/G** | **D6** | **C6/G** |
| **D6** | **Dm7 G9** | **G6** | **Cmaj9** :‖ *Repeat and fade*

Catch a Wave

Words and Music by
Brian Wilson and Mike Love

Melody:

Catch a wave and you're sit - tin' on

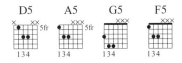

D5	A5	G5	F5

N.C.

Intro
  Catch a wave and you're sittin' on top of the world.

D5

Verse 1
  Don't be afraid to try the greatest sport around.
A5   **D5**
  Those who don't just have to put it down.
G5
  You paddle out, turn around and raise and, baby,
D5
  That's all there is to the coastline craze.
      A5 **F5**
You gotta catch a wave
      G5 **A5**   **D5**
And you're sittin' on top of the world.

D5

Verse 2
  Not just a fad 'cause it's been goin' on so long.
A5   **D5**
  They said it wouldn't last too long.
G5
  They'll eat their words with a fork and spoon.
      D5
And watch 'em, they'll hit the road

And all be surfin' soon.
      A5 **F5**
And when they catch a wave,
      G5 **A5**   **D5**
They'll be sittin' on top of the world.

Copyright © 1963 IRVING MUSIC, INC.
Copyright Renewed
All Rights Reserved   Used by Permission

Interlude

```
| A5       |        | D5    |      |     |
| A5       |        | D5    |      |     |
| G5       |        | D5    |      |     |
  A5    F5          G5    A5          D5
```

Catch a wave and you're sittin' on top of the world.

Verse 3

D5

So take a lesson from a top notch surfer boy.

A5   **D5**

But don't you treat it like a toy.

G5

Just get away from the shady turf,

          D5

And, baby,   go catch some rays on the sunny surf.

             A5   **F5**

And when you   catch a wave

           G5   **A5**   **D5**

You'll be sittin' on top of the world.

Outro

    A5   **F5**

‖:   Catch a wave, you'll be

G5   **A5**   **D5**

Sittin' on top of the world.   :‖ *Repeat and fade*

Cherry Cherry Coupe

Words and Music by
Brian Wilson and Roger Christian

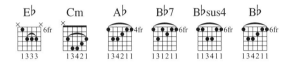

Eb	Cm	Ab	Bb7	Bbsus4	Bb

Intro

    Eb   Cm
Go, cherry cherry coupe now.

Verse 1

         Eb   Cm
The wildest short around is my cherry, cherry coupe.

         Eb   Cm
The sharpest in the town and the envy of my group.

        Ab
It's one of it's kind and it really looks good.

         Bb7
Chopped nose and decked with lovers on the hood.

Chorus 1

    Eb   Cm
Go, cherry cherry coupe now.

    Eb   Cm
Go, cherry cherry coupe now.

    Ab
Go, cherry cherry coupe now.

          Bb7   Bbsus4 Bb
Why don't you go, cherry, cherry coupe   now.

Copyright © 1964 IRVING MUSIC, INC. and CAREERS-BMG MUSIC PUBLISHING, INC. for the USA
Copyright Renewed
All Rights outside the USA Controlled by IRVING MUSIC, INC.
All Rights Reserved   Used by Permission

Verse 2

        E♭   Cm
My chrome reverse wheels and whitewall slicks,

          E♭   Cm
And it turns a quarter mile in a one-o six.

          A♭
Door handles are off but you know I'll never miss 'em.

          B♭7
They open when I want with a solenoid system.

Chorus 2

Repeat Chorus 1

Verse 3

        E♭   Cm
My coupe's tuck and roll under-neath the hood,

          E♭   Cm
And the rugs, seats, and panels now are lookin' good.

          A♭
When I go lookin' for somethin' to do,

          B♭7
It's got enough room now to barely seat two.

Outro

Repeat Chorus 1 till fade

Country Air

Words and Music by
Brian Wilson and Mike Love

Melody:

Get a breath of that coun-try air. __

Bm   F#7   D   Dsus4   F#   G   A

Intro

Bm	F#7	Bm	F#7
D	Dsus4	D	Dsus4
F#	G	F#	G

Verse 1

    D   **A**
Get a breath of that country air.

    D   **A**
Breathe the beauty of it ev'rywhere.

    D   **G**
Get a look at that clear blue sky.

| Bm | F#7 | Bm | F#7 |

Interlude 1

| D | Dsus4 | D | Dsus4 |
| F# | G | F# | G |

Copyright © 1968 IRVING MUSIC, INC.
Copyright Renewed
All Rights Reserved   Used by Permission

Verse 2

D   A
Get a breath of that country air.

D   A
Breathe the beauty of it ev'rywhere.

D   G
Mother Nature, she fills __ my eyes.

| Bm | F♯7 | Bm | F♯7 | |

Interlude 2

Repeat Interlude 1

Verse 3

D   A
Get a breath of that country air.

D   A
Breathe the beauty of it ev'rywhere.

D   G   Bm F♯7 G   A7
Rise up, beauty, the day __ won't let you sleep.

Outro

D   A7
(Ah, ha.

D   A7
Ah, ha.

D   G Bm F#7 Bm F♯7
Ah, ha.)   *Fade out*

Custom Machine

Words and Music by
Brian Wilson and Mike Love

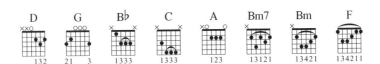

Intro

N.C.
Check my custom machine.

Verse 1

    D   G
Well, she's metal flake blue with a Corvette grill.

B♭ C   A
Check my custom ma-chine.

     D   G
And they say it looks better when she's standin' still.

Chorus 1

C   A   D
Check my custom ma-chine.
      (When I step on the gas, she goes…)

Bm7
Wa.

  D Bm   G   C   F A
I'll let you look, but don't __ touch my custom machine.

Copyright © 1964 IRVING MUSIC, INC.
Copyright Renewed
All Rights Reserved   Used by Permission

Verse 2

          D   **G**
Well, with naugahyde bucket seats in front and back.

Bb   **C**   **A**
Check my custom ma-chine.

       D   **G**
Ev'ry-thing is chromed, man, even my jack.

Chorus 2

Repeat Chorus 1

Verse 3

          D   **G**
A stereophonic speaker set with vibrasonic sound.

Bb   **C**   **A**
Check my custom ma-chine.

       D   **G**
Mag-nesium spokes, and stands an inch off the ground.

Chorus 3

Repeat Chorus 1

Outro

‖: **A** | :‖ *Repeat and fade*

Dance, Dance, Dance

Words and Music by
Brian Wilson, Carl Wilson and Mike Love

Melody:

Af - ter   six hours of   school _ I've had   e -

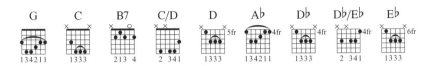

G	C	B7	C/D	D	A♭	D♭	D♭/E♭	E♭

Verse 1

N.C.(G7)
After six hours of school

I've had enough for the day.

I hit the radio dial

And turn it up all the way.

Chorus 1

      G   **C**
I gotta dance right on the spot.

          G
This beat's really hot.

B7   **C**   **C/D**   **D**
Dance, dance, dance, yeah.

Copyright © 1964 IRVING MUSIC, INC.
Copyright Renewed
All Rights Reserved   Used by Permission

Verse 2

N.C.(G7)
When I feel put down

I try to shake it off quick.

With my chick by my side,

The radio does the trick.

Chorus 2

       G   **C**
I love to dance right on the spot.
               G
This beat's really hot.
B7   **C**   **C/D**   **D**
Dance, dance, dance, yeah. (Oh, my.)

Guitar Solo

G				
C		**G**		
B7	**C**	**C/D**	**D**	

Verse 3

N.C.(G7)
At a weekend dance,

We like to show up last.

(A♭)
I play it cool when it's slow

And jump in when it's fast.

Chorus 3

          A♭   **D♭**
I love to dance right on the spot.

                   A♭
This beat's really hot.

C   **D♭**   **D♭/E♭** **E♭**
Dance, dance, dance,   yeah.

Outro

      A♭
‖: Dance, dance, dance,

Now the beat's really hot.
D♭
Dance, dance, dance,

Right there on the spot.
A♭
Dance, dance, dance,

Now the beat's really hot.
C   **D♭**   **D♭/E♭** **E♭**
Dance, dance, dance, yeah. :‖ ***Repeat and fade***

Darlin'

Words and Music by
Brian Wilson and Mike Love

Melody:

Oh,   dar - lin'

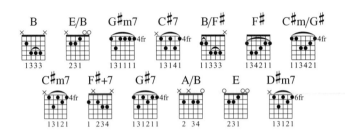

B   E/B   G#m7   C#7   B/F#   F#   C#m/G#

C#m7   F#+7   G#7   A/B   E   D#m7

Intro

    B **E/B**
Oh, d-d-d-darlin', oo, oo,

  G#m7   **C#7**
My darlin', you're so fine.

B/F# **F#** **C#m/G#** **B** **F#**
Oh.

Verse 1

      C#m7
You know if words could say,

F#   **C#m7**
 But darlin', I'll find a way

F#   **B**
 To let you know what you meant to me.

F#+7   **B**
 Guess it was meant to be.

G#7   **C#m7**
 I hold you in my heart

F#   **C#m7**
 As life's most precious part.

Copyright © 1968 IRVING MUSIC, INC.
Copyright Renewed
All Rights Reserved   Used by Permission

	B
Chorus 1	Oh, dar - lin',

E/B
I dream about you often.

G♯m7
My pretty darlin',

C♯7
I love the way you soften

B/F♯
My life with your love,

       F♯   **C♯m/G♯**   **B**   **F♯**
Your pre - cious love, a-huh.   Oh.

	C♯m7
Verse 2	I was livin' like half a man.

F♯   **C♯m7**
  Then I couldn't love, but now I can.

F♯   **B**
  You pick me up when I'm feelin' sad,

F♯+7   **B**
  More so than I ever had.

G♯7   **C♯m7**
  Gonna love you ev'ry single night,

F♯   **C♯m7**   **F♯**
  'Cause I think you're too out of sight.

Chorus 2

        B
Oh, dar - lin',

E/B
I dream about you often.

  G♯m7
My pretty darlin',

 C♯7
I love the way you soften

  B/F♯
My life with your love,

    F♯
Your pre - cious love, a-huh.

| **C♯m/G♯** | **A/B** | **E** | **F♯** | **A/B** | |

Bridge

E   **F♯**   **A/B** **E** **F♯**
Every night, __ whoa, dar - lin'.

       C♯m7
Gonna love you ev'ry single night.

   D♯m7
Yes, I will.

         E   **F♯**
'Cause I think you're too doggone out of sight.

Chorus 3   *Repeat Chorus 1 till fade*

THE BEACH BOYS

Do It Again

Words and Music by
Brian Wilson and Mike Love

Melody:

It's au - to - mat - ic when I

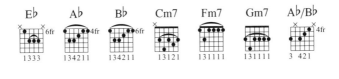

Eb Ab Bb Cm7 Fm7 Gm7 Ab/Bb

Intro

| Eb | | | | |

Verse 1

      Eb
It's automatic when I talk with old friends

And conversation turns to girls we knew
      Ab   **Bb**
When their hair was soft and long,
              Eb
And the beach was the place to go.

Verse 2

      Eb
The suntanned bodies and the waves of sunshine.

The California girls and a beautiful coastline,
     Ab
And warmed up weather, let's
Bb   **Eb**
  Get together and do it again.

Copyright © 1968 IRVING MUSIC, INC.
Copyright Renewed
All Rights Reserved   Used by Permission

Interlude 1 | E♭ | | | |
  | A♭ | B♭ | E♭ | |

Bridge

A♭　　　　　　　　　Cm7　　　　　Fm7
With a girl the lonely sea looks good with moonlight.

A♭　　　　Gm7　　　　　A♭/B♭
Makes your nighttimes warm and out of sight.

  | B♭ | | | |

Interlude 2 | E♭ | | | |
  | A♭ | B♭ | E♭ | |

Verse 3

E♭
Well, I've been thinkin' 'bout all the places

We've surfed and danced, and all the faces we've

A♭
Missed. So let's get

B♭　　　　　　　E♭
Back together and do it again.

Outro ‖: E♭ | | | |
  | A♭ | B♭ | E♭ | :‖ *Repeat and fade*

THE BEACH BOYS

Do You Remember?

Words and Music by
Brian Wilson and Mike Love

Lit - tle Rich - ard sang it and

F7   C   G7

Verse 1

F7
Little Richard sang it and

              C
Dick Clark brought it to life.

F7
Danny and the Juniors hit a groove,

           C
Stuck as sharp as a knife.

       G7
Well, now, do you remember all the

                 C
Guys that gave us rock and roll?

Verse 2

F7
Chuck Berry's gotta be the

           C
Greatest thing that came a-long.

F7
He made the guitar beats and

           C
Wrote the all-time greatest songs.

      G7
Well, now, do you remember all the

              C
Guys that gave us rock and roll?

Copyright © 1964 IRVING MUSIC, INC.
Copyright Renewed
All Rights Reserved   Used by Permission

Bridge

       F7
Elvis Presley is the king,

He's the giant of our day.

       C
He paved the way for the rock and roll stars.

      F7
Yet the critics kept a knockin',

And the stars kept a rockin',

     G7
And their choppin' didn't get very far.

Verse 3

F7
Nothin's really movin'

           C
Till the saxophone is ready to blow.

F7
And the beat's not jumpin'

           C
Till the drummer says he's ready to go.

     G7
Well, now, do you remember

           C
All the guys that gave us rock and roll?

Don't Back Down

Words and Music by
Brian Wilson and Mike Love

Melody:

The girls dig the way the guys get

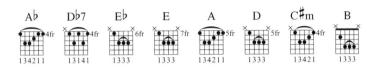

Ab   Db7   Eb   E   A   D   C#m   B

Verse 1

                 Ab
The girls dig the way the guys get all wiped out,

With their feet in the air you can hear 'em shout.

         Db7
They're not a-fraid,

       Ab
Not my boys.

      Eb
They grit their teeth;

                E
They don't back down.

Chorus 1

A   **D**   **E**   **A**
Oo, you gotta be a little nuts.

   D   **E**   **A**
But show 'em now who's got guts.

   D   **E**   **D**   **C#m**   **B**
Don't __ back down __ from that wave.

Copyright © 1964 IRVING MUSIC, INC.
Copyright Renewed
All Rights Reserved   Used by Permission

GUITAR CHORD SONGBOOK

Verse 2

A♭
With their feet full of tar, and their hair full of sand,

The boys know the surf like the palm of their hand.

D♭7
They're not a-fraid,

A♭
Not my boys.

E♭
They grit their teeth;

E
They don't back down.

Chorus 2 *Repeat Chorus 1*

Verse 3

A♭
When a twenty-footer sneaks up like a ton of lead,

And the crest comes along and slaps 'em upside the head,

D♭7
They're not a-fraid,

A♭
Not my boys.

E♭
They grit their teeth;

E
They don't back down.

Chorus 3

A
Don't back down.

D   **E**   **A**
You gotta be a little nuts.

D   **E**   **A**
But show 'em now   who's got guts.

D   **E**   **D** **C♯m** **B**
Don't __ back down from that wave.

Outro

A   **D** **E**
‖: Don't back down.   :‖ *Repeat and fade*

Don't Talk

Words and Music by
Brian Wilson and Tony Asher

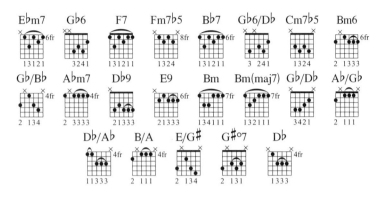

Verse 1

> **E♭m7**   **G♭6**   **F7**
> I can hear so much in your sighs,
>
> **Fm7♭5**   **B♭7**   **G♭6/D♭**   **Cm7♭5**
> And I can see so much in your eyes.
>
> **Bm6**   **G♭/B♭**   **A♭m7**
> There are words we both could say.

Chorus 1

> **D♭9**
> But don't talk,
>
>   **A♭m7**
> Put your head on my shoulder.
>
> **D♭9**
> Come close,
>
>   **A♭m7**
> Close your eyes and be still.
>
> **E9**
> Don't talk,
>
>   **Bm**   **Bm(maj7)**   **Bm6**   **E9**   **G♭/D♭**
> Take my hand and let me hear your heart   beat.

Copyright © 1966 IRVING MUSIC, INC.
Copyright Renewed
All Rights Reserved   Used by Permission

Verse 2

E♭m7   **G♭6**   **F7**
Being here with you feels so right;

Fm7♭5   **B♭7**   **G♭6/D♭**   **Cm7♭5**
We could live for-ever   to-night.

Bm6   **G♭/B♭**   **A♭m7**
Let's not think about to-morrow.

Chorus 2

D♭9
And don't talk,

      A♭m7
Put your head on my shoulder.

D♭9
Come close,

       A♭m7
Close your eyes and be still.

E9
Don't talk,

      Bm   **Bm(maj7)** **Bm6** **E9**
Take my hand and listen to my heart.

G♭/D♭
Please listen, listen,

Interlude

| **E♭m7 A♭/G♭** | **D♭/A♭ B/A** | **E/G♯ G♯°7** |
listen.

| **G♭/B♭ Bm6** | **D♭** | |

Outro

D♭9
‖:   Don't talk,

      A♭m7
Put your head on my shoulder.

D♭9
Don't talk,

      A♭m7
Close your eyes and be still. :‖ ***Repeat and fade***

Don't Worry Baby

Words and Music by
Brian Wilson and Roger Christian

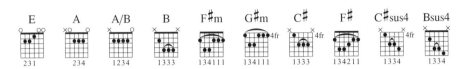

Well, it's been build-ing up in-side of me for, __

E	A	A/B	B	F#m	G#m	C#	F#	C#sus4	Bsus4
231	234	1234	1333	134111	134111	1333	134211	1334	1334

Intro   ‖: E | | A | A/B :‖
           (Ah.)

Verse 1

   E
     Well, it's been building up inside of me

    A   B
For, __ oh, I don't know __ how long.

   E
     I don't know why, but I keep thinking

 A   B
Something's bound to __ go wrong.

 F#m   B
    But she looks in my eyes

 G#m   C#
    And makes me realize

Chorus 1

        F#
When she __ says,

        G#m
"Don't worry, ba - by.

C#sus4 C#   F#
   Ev'ry-thing will turn out __ all right.

       G#m
Don't worry, ba - by."

C#sus4 C# Bsus4 B
    Oo,   oo.

Copyright © 1964 IRVING MUSIC, INC. and CAREERS-BMG MUSIC PUBLISHING, INC. for the USA
Copyright Renewed
All Rights outside the USA Controlled by IRVING MUSIC, INC.
All Rights Reserved   Used by Permission

Verse 2

E
I guess I should have kept my mouth shut

       A   B
When I'd __ start to brag a-bout my car.

E
But I can't back down now

       A   B
Because I __ pushed the other guys too far.

F♯m   B
She makes me come alive

G♯m   C♯
And makes me wanna drive...

Chorus 2   *Repeat Chorus 1*

Interlude   ‖: E | | A | A/B :‖

Verse 3

E
She told me, "Baby, when you race today,

     A   B
Just __ take along my __ love with you.

E
And if you knew how much I love you,

      A   B
Baby, __ nothing could go __ wrong with you."

F♯m   B
Oh, what she does to me

G♯m   C♯
When she makes love to me...

Outro

       F♯
And she __ says,

          G♯m
‖: "Don't worry, ba - by.

C♯sus4 C♯   F♯
Ev'ry-thing will turn out __ all right. :‖ ***Repeat and fade***

Drive In

Words and Music by
Brian Wilson and Mike Love

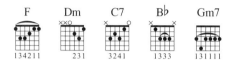

F   Dm   C7   B♭   Gm7

Verse 1

      F
Ev'ry time I have a date there's only one place to go,

        Dm
That's to the drive-in.

     F
It's such a pretty place to talk, and maybe watch a show

     C7
Down at the drive-in.

   B♭
For-get about the plot, it'll do very well.

      F
But make sure you see enough

So you're prepared to tell
    Gm7
About the drive-in.

C7   **F**
   I love the drive-in.

Copyright © 1964 IRVING MUSIC, INC.
Copyright Renewed
All Rights Reserved   Used by Permission

Verse 2

       F
If the windows get fogged it's time to take a breath

    Dm
Down at the drive-in.

     F
Or the cat dressed in white'll scare you both to death

    C7
Down at the drive-in.

  B♭
A big buttered popcorn and an extra large Coke,

  F
A few chili dogs and man, I'm goin' broke,

     Gm7
Down at the drive-in.

C7   **F**
   I love the drive-in.

Verse 3

          F
Don't sneak your buddies in the trunk 'cause they might get caught

    Dm
By the drive-in.

     F
And they'd look kind of stupid gettin' chased through the lot

    C7
Around the drive-in.

   B♭
If you say you watched the movie, you're a couple of liars,

    F
And re-member only you can prevent forest fires,

     Gm7
Down at the drive-in.

C7   **F**
   I love the drive-in.

409

Words and Music by
Brian Wilson, Gary Usher and Mike Love

Melody:

She's real fine, my four - o - nine.

G   C   D7   C7

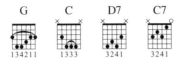

134211 1333 3241 3241

Intro

N.C.
She's real fine, my four-o-nine.

She's real fine, my four-o-nine,

      G
My four-o-nine.

Verse 1

G
Well, I saved my pennies and I saved my dimes.

(Giddy-up, giddy-up four-o-nine.)
C
For I knew there would be a time
G
(Giddy-up, giddy-up four-o-nine.)
    D7   **C7**   **G**
When I would buy a brand ___ new four-o-nine.

Copyright © 1962 IRVING MUSIC, INC.
Copyright Renewed
All Rights Reserved   Used by Permission

Chorus 1

G
Giddy-up, giddy-up, giddy-up four-o-nine.

C
Giddy-up four-o-nine.

G
Giddy-up four-o-nine.

Giddy-up four-o...
D7
Nothing can catch her,

C7   **G**
Nothing can touch my four-o-nine, four-o-nine.

Guitar Solo

G
(Oo, giddy-up, giddy-up.

Oo, giddy-up, giddy-up.
C
Oo, giddy-up, giddy-up.

G   **D7**   **C7**   **G**
Oo, giddy-up, giddy-up.)

Verse 2

G
When I take her to the drag, she really shines.

(Giddy-up, giddy-up four-o-nine.)
C
She always turns in the fastest time.

G
(Giddy-up, giddy-up four-o-nine.)
D7   **C7**   **G**
My four-speed, dual quad, posi-traction four-o-nine.

Chorus 2   *Repeat Chorus 1*

Outro

G
‖: Giddy-up four-o-nine.   :‖ *Repeat and fade*

Friends

Words and Music by Brian Wilson,
Carl Wilson, Dennis Wilson and Al Jardine

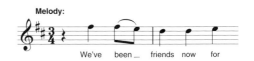

Melody:

We've been _ friends now for

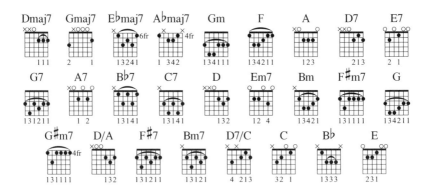

Verse 1

> **Dmaj7**   **Gmaj7**
> We've been friends now for
>
> **Dmaj7** **Gmaj7**
> So many years.
>
> **E♭maj7**   **A♭maj7**
> We've been to-gether
>
>   **E♭maj7**   **A♭maj7**
> Through the good times and the tears.
>
>   **Gm**   **F**   **Gm**
> Turned each other on to the good things that
>
> **F**   **A**
> Life has to give.

Interlude 1 | D7 | E7 | G7 | A7 B♭7 C7 | D | |

Copyright © 1968 IRVING MUSIC, INC.
Copyright Renewed
All Rights Reserved   Used by Permission

Verse 2

    Dmaj7   **Gmaj7**
We drift a-part

      Dmaj7   **Gmaj7**
For a little bit of a spell.

     E♭maj7   **A♭maj7**
One night I get a call

     E♭maj7   **A♭maj7**
And I know that you're well.

    Gm   **F**
And days I was down you would

Gm   **F**   **A**
Help me get out of my hole.

Interlude 2 | D7 | E7 | G7 | A7 B♭7 C7 | D | |

Bridge | Em7 | Bm | Em7 | A7 |
     (Ah.)

    | D | F♯m7 | G |

G♯m7   **D/A**
  Let's be friends,

F♯7   **Bm7**
  Let's be friends,

D7/C   **Gmaj7**   **A7**
  Let's be friends.

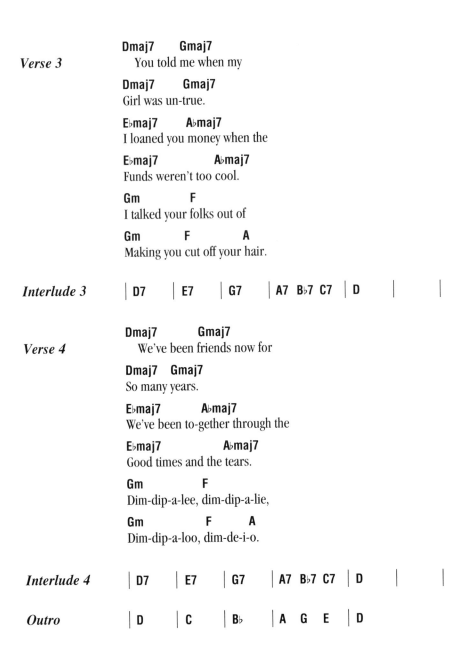

Verse 3

Dmaj7   Gmaj7
  You told me when my

Dmaj7   Gmaj7
Girl was un-true.

E♭maj7   A♭maj7
I loaned you money when the

E♭maj7   A♭maj7
Funds weren't too cool.

Gm   F
I talked your folks out of

Gm   F   A
Making you cut off your hair.

Interlude 3

| D7 | E7 | G7 | A7 B♭7 C7 | D | | |

Verse 4

Dmaj7   Gmaj7
  We've been friends now for

Dmaj7 Gmaj7
So many years.

E♭maj7   A♭maj7
We've been to-gether through the

E♭maj7   A♭maj7
Good times and the tears.

Gm   F
Dim-dip-a-lee, dim-dip-a-lie,

Gm   F   A
Dim-dip-a-loo, dim-de-i-o.

Interlude 4

| D7 | E7 | G7 | A7 B♭7 C7 | D | | |

Outro

| D | C | B♭ | A G E | D |

Fun, Fun, Fun

Words and Music by
Brian Wilson and Mike Love

Melody:

Well, she got her dad-dy's car...

(Tune down 1/2 step)

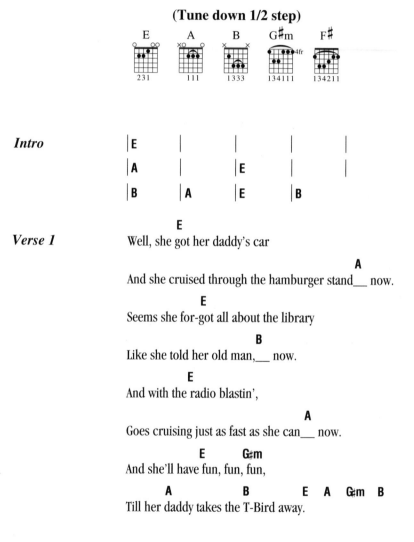

E   A   B   G#m   F#

Intro

E				
A		E		
B	A	E	B

Verse 1

         E
Well, she got her daddy's car

                      A
And she cruised through the hamburger stand__ now.

        E
Seems she for-got all about the library

           B
Like she told her old man,__ now.

      E
And with the radio blastin',

               A
Goes cruising just as fast as she can__ now.

      E   **G#m**
And she'll have fun, fun, fun,

    A   **B**   **E** **A** **G#m** **B**
Till her daddy takes the T-Bird away.

Copyright © 1964 IRVING MUSIC, INC.
Copyright Renewed
All Rights Reserved   Used by Permission

Verse 2

```
                    E
Well, the girls can't stand her
                                                    A
'Cause she walks, looks, and drives like an ace__ now.
                    E
She makes the Indy 500 look like
                          B
A Roman chariot race__ now.
                    E
A lotta guys try to catch her,
                                              A
But she leads them on a wild goose chase__ now.
                    E        G#m
And she'll have fun, fun, fun,
              A              B          E   A  G#m  B
Till her daddy takes the T-Bird away.
```

Verse 3

```
                    E
Well, you knew all along
                                        A
That your dad was gettin' wise to you__ now.
                    E
And since he took your set of keys
                                              B
You've been thinking that your fun is all through__ now.
                    E
But you can come along with me,
                                  A
'Cause we gotta lotta things to do__ now.
                    E      G#m
And we'll have fun, fun, fun,
              A              B          E   A  G#m  B
Till her daddy takes the T-Bird away.
```

Outro

        E   **G♯m**
And we'll have fun, fun, fun,

      A   **B**   **E** **A** **G♯m** **B**
Now that daddy took the T-Bird away.

        E   **G♯m**
And we'll have fun, fun, fun,

      A   **B**   **E** **A** **G♯m** **F♯**
Now that daddy took the T-Bird away.

   B
‖: (Fun, fun, fun,

                  E
Now that Daddy took the T-Bird away.

Fun, fun, fun,

   A
Now that Daddy took the T-Bird away.) :‖ *Repeat and fade*

Girl Don't Tell Me

Words and Music by Brian Wilson

Melody:

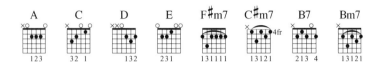

Hi, lit - tle girl, it's me. ___ Don't you know

A   C   D   E   F#m7   C#m7   B7   Bm7

Verse 1

```
     A              C
Hi, little girl, it's me.
          D          A
Don't you know who I am?

I met you last summer when I
C           D        A
Came up to stay __ with my gran.
        E      A          E
I'm the guy ___ who left ___ you
          A           E
With tears in his eyes.
            F#m7      C#m7
You didn't answer my letter
     F#m7        A      B7    D
So I figured it was __ just a lie.
```

Copyright © 1965 IRVING MUSIC, INC.
Copyright Renewed
All Rights Reserved   Used by Permission

Verse 2

    A
Your hair's getting longer and your

C   **D**   **A**
Shorts, mm, they sure fit you fine.

I'll bet you went out ev'ry

C   **D**   **A**
Night during __ good ol' school time.

         E   **A**
But this a time

        E   **A**   **E**
I'm not __ gonna count on you.

    F♯m7   **C♯m7**
I'll see you this summer

      F♯m7   **A**   **Bm7**   **D**
And for-get you when I __ go back to school.

Outro

Bm7   **C♯m7**   **F♯m7** **C♯m7**
Girl, don't tell me you'll write.

Bm7   **C♯m7**   **D** **F♯m7**
Girl, don't tell me you'll write.

Bm7   **C♯m7**
Girl, don't tell me you'll

    F♯m7   **E**   **A**
Write __ me again __ this time.

Girls on the Beach

Words and Music by
Brian Wilson and Mike Love

Melody:

On the beach you'll find them there,

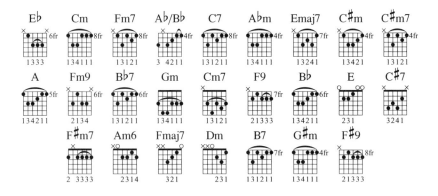

Eb   Cm   Fm7   Ab/Bb   C7   Abm   Emaj7   C#m   C#m7

A   Fm9   Bb7   Gm   Cm7   F9   Bb   E   C#7

F#m7   Am6   Fmaj7   Dm   B7   G#m   F#9

Verse 1

  Eb   Cm   Fm7   Ab/Bb
On the beach you'll find them there,

Eb   C7   Fm7 Abm
In the sun and salty air.

   Emaj7   C#m   Emaj7   C#m7
The girls on the beach are all within reach,

    A   Fm9   Bb7
If you know what to do.

Verse 2

  Eb   Cm   Fm7   Ab/Bb
How we love to lie   a-round

Eb   C7   Fm7   Abm
Girls with tans of golden brown.

   Emaj7   C#m   Emaj7   C#m7
The girls on the beach are all within reach,

    A   Fm9
And one waits there for you.

Copyright © 1964 IRVING MUSIC, INC.
Copyright Renewed
All Rights Reserved   Used by Permission

Bridge

Bb7   Eb   Emaj7   Eb
Girls on the beach.

   Gm   Cm7
The sun in her hair,

   Gm   Cm7
The warmth of the air,

    F9   Fm7   Bb7
On a summer day

Eb   Cm   Fm7   Bb
As the sun dips out of sight.

Verse 3

E   C#7   F#m7   Am6
Couples on the beach at night.

   Fmaj7   Dm   Fmaj7   Dm
The girls on the beach are all within reach,

   Bb   B7
And with the boys to-night,

        E   C#m   A   Fmaj7
Girls on the beach.

Outro

   E   G#m
‖: Girls on the beach,

C#m7   F#9
Girls on the beach.   :‖ *Repeat and fade*

God Only Knows

Words and Music by
Brian Wilson and Tony Asher

Melody:

I may not al-ways love _ you,

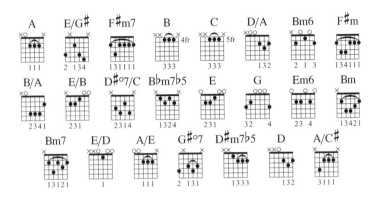

Intro

‖: A | E/G♯ :‖ *Play 3 times*

| F♯m7 | A   B   C |

Verse 1

D/A   Bm6
I may not always love you,

F♯m   F♯m7   B/A
But long as there are ___ stars above you,

E/B   D♯°7/C
You never need to doubt it.

E/B   B♭m7♭5
I'll make you so ___ sure about it.

Chorus 1

A   E/G♯
God only knows

              F♯m7   E   F♯m7 G
What I'd be without ___ you.

Copyright © 1966 IRVING MUSIC, INC.
Copyright Renewed
All Rights Reserved   Used by Permission

Verse 2

   D/A   **Bm6**
   If you should ever leave me,

F♯m   **F♯m7**   **B/A**
Well, life would still go ____ on, believe me.

E/B   **D♯°7/C**
The world could show nothing to me,

E/B   **B♭m7♭5**
So what good would ____ living do me.

Chorus 2

A   **E/G♯**
God only knows

               F♯m7   **N.C.**
What I'd be without ____ you.

Interlude

| G | Em6 | Bm Bm7 | E/D | |
| A/E | G♯°7 | A/E | D♯m7♭5 | |

Chorus 3

    D   **A/C♯**
And God only knows

           Bm7
What I'd be without ____ you.

Verse 3

Repeat Verse 2

Chorus 4

A   **E/G♯**
God only knows

          F♯m7   **E/G♯**
What I'd be without ____ you.

Outro

   A   **E/G♯**
‖: And God only knows

         F♯m7   **E/G♯**
What I'd be without ____ you. :‖ ***Repeat and fade***

Good Vibrations

Words and Music by
Brian Wilson and Mike Love

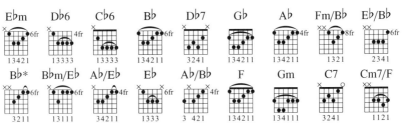

Verse 1

       E♭m   **D♭6**
I, ____ I love the colorful clothes she wears,

        C♭6   **B♭**
And the way the sunlight plays upon her hair.

E♭m   **D♭6**
I hear the sound of a gentle word,

      C♭6   **B♭**   **D♭7**
On the wind that lifts her perfume through the air.

Chorus 1

      G♭
      I'm pickin' up good vibrations.

She's givin' me the excitations.

I'm pickin' up good vibrations.

She's givin' me the excitations.

     A♭
     I'm pickin' up good vibrations.

She's givin' me the excitations.

B♭
     I'm pickin' up good vibrations.

She's givin' me the excitations.

Copyright © 1966 IRVING MUSIC, INC.
Copyright Renewed
All Rights Reserved   Used by Permission

Verse 2	E♭m D♭6

Verse 2

E♭m   D♭6
Close my eyes, she's somehow closer now.

C♭6   B♭
Softly smile, I know she must be kind.

E♭m   D♭6
When I look in her eyes

         C♭6   B♭   D♭7
She goes with me to a blossom room.

Chorus 2   *Repeat Chorus 1*

Bridge   ‖: Fm/B♭   E♭/B♭ | B♭*   E♭/B♭ :‖ *Play 5 times*

   Fm/B♭   E♭/B♭
(Oh,   my,

B♭*   E♭/B♭
My one ____ elation.)

   B♭m/E♭   A♭/E♭
I don't know where,

             E♭   A♭/E♭
But she sends __ me there.

B♭m/E♭   A♭/E♭ E♭   A♭/B♭
        My,   my one __ sensation.

Fm/B♭   E♭/B♭ B♭*   E♭/B♭
Oh,   my,   my one elation.

Fm/B♭   E♭/B♭ B♭*   E♭/B♭
My,   my,   my one...

Interlude | F | | Gm | C7 |

Verse 3

F

  Gotta keep those lovin' good

Gm   C7

  Vibrations a happenin' with her.

F

  Gotta keep those lovin' good

Gm   C7

  Vibrations a happenin' with her.

F

  Gotta keep those lovin' good

Gm   C7

  Vibrations a happenin' with her.

| F | | | Gm | C7 | |
| F | | | Cm7/F | N.C. | |

Chorus 3

B♭

  I'm pickin' up good vibrations.

She's givin' me the excitations.

A♭   G♭

Good, good, good, good vibrations.

Outro

G♭

Na, na, na, na, na,

Na, na, na.

A♭

Na, na, na, na, na,

Na, na, na.

B♭

Na, na, na, na, na,

Na, na, na.

A♭

Na, na, na, na, na,

Na, na, na.

‖: A♭ | :‖ *Repeat and fade*

Help Me Rhonda

Words and Music by
Brian Wilson and Mike Love

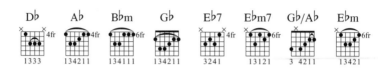

Db	Ab	Bbm	Gb	Eb7	Ebm7	Gb/Ab	Ebm
1333	134211	134111	134211	3241	13121	3 4211	13421

Verse 1

                Db
Well, since she put me down

             Ab   **Db**
I've been out doin' in my head.

I come in late at night

             Ab   **Db**
And in the mornin' I just lay in bed.

Pre-Chorus 1

            Bbm
Well, Rhonda you look so fine,

        Gb   **Eb7**
And I know it wouldn't take much time

             Db
For you to   help me, Rhonda,

        Ebm7   **Db**
Help __ me get her out of my heart.

Copyright © 1965 IRVING MUSIC, INC.
Copyright Renewed
All Rights Reserved   Used by Permission

Chorus 1

A♭
Help me, Rhonda, help, help me, Rhonda.

D♭
Help me, Rhonda, help, help me, Rhonda.

A♭
Help me, Rhonda, help, help me, Rhonda.

D♭
Help me, Rhonda, help, help me, Rhonda.

G♭
Help me, Rhonda, help, help me, Rhonda.

B♭m   **D♭**
Help me, Rhonda, help, __ help me, Rhonda.

E♭m7   **A♭**   **N.C.**
Help me, Rhonda, yeah.

                     D♭
Get her out of my heart.

Verse 2

     D♭
She was gonna be my wife

     G♭/A♭   **D♭**   **E♭m7**
And I ___ was gonna be her man.

D♭
   But she let another guy come

     G♭/A♭   **D♭**   **E♭m7 D♭**
Be-tween us and it shattered our plans.

Pre-Chorus 2

B♭m
Well, Rhonda, you caught my eye,

G♭   E♭7
And I could give you lots of reasons why

D♭
You gotta   help me, Rhonda,

E♭m7   D♭
Help ____ me get her out of my heart.

Chorus 2   *Repeat Chorus 1*

Interlude

D♭				
G♭		D♭		
E♭m	G♭	D♭		

Chorus 3   *Repeat Chorus 1*

Outro   ‖: D♭ | :‖   *Repeat and fade*

Hawaii

Words and Music by
Brian Wilson and Mike Love

Melody:

Go to Ha - wai - i, _____

C   F   Dm   G7   Am   D   D+   G

32 1   1 34211   2 3 1   3 2 1   2 3 1   1 3 2   2 3 1   2 1   3

Chorus 1

       C
Go to Ha-waii, Hawaii,

      F C
Straight to Ha-waii.

     Dm G7   **C**
Oh, do you wanna come along with me?

Verse 1

     F
  I've heard about all the perty girls

      C
With their grass skirts down to their knees.

       Am
All my life __ I've wanted

     D   **D+** **D** **G**
To see __ the island called Hawai - i.

Copyright © 1964 IRVING MUSIC, INC.
Copyright Renewed
All Rights Reserved   Used by Permission

GUITAR CHORD SONGBOOK

Chorus 2   *Repeat Chorus 1*

Verse 2
      F
      Now, I don't know what town you're from,

         C
But don't tell me that they got bigger waves.

              Am
'Cause ev'ryone __ that goes

        D   **D+**   **D**   **G**
Comes back __ with nothin' but raves.

Chorus 3
           C
That's in Ha-waii, Hawaii,

         F C
Straight to Ha-waii.

        Dm   **G7**   **C**
Oh, do you wanna come along with me?

Verse 3
      F
      And perty soon this summer they'll

         C
Hold the surfin' championship of the year.

              Am
Surfer guys __ and girls

        D   **D+ D**   **G**
Will be com - in' from far and near.

Chorus 4   *Repeat Chorus 1*

Here Today

Words and Music by
Brian Wilson and Tony Asher

Melody:

It starts with just ___ a lit-tle glance ___ now,

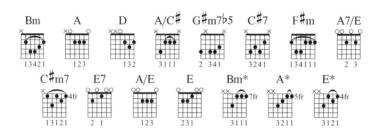

Bm   A   D   A/C♯   G♯m7♭5   C♯7   F♯m   A7/E

C♯m7   E7   A/E   E   Bm*   A*   E*

Verse 1

Bm
It starts with just a little glance now,

A
Right away you're thinkin' 'bout romance now.

Bm
You know you ought to take it slower,

A
But you just can't wait to get to know her.

D   **A/C♯**   **Bm   A   G♯m7♭5**
A brand new   love af - fair

C♯7   **F♯m**   **A7/E**
Is such a beautiful thing.

D   **A/C♯**   **Bm   A**
But if you're not   care - ful,

G♯m7♭5   **C♯7**   **F♯m**
Think ___ about the pain it can bring.

Copyright © 1966 IRVING MUSIC, INC.
Copyright Renewed
All Rights Reserved   Used by Permission

Pre-Chorus 1

         C♯7
It makes you feel so bad,

          F♯m
It makes your heart feel sad.

         C♯7
It makes your days go wrong,

         C♯m7
It makes your nights so long.

         E7
You've got to keep in mind

Chorus 1

        A   D A/E   D
Love is here   today

   E   A   D A/E   D
And it's gone   tomor - row.

E   A   D   E7
It's here __ and gone so fast.

Verse 2

Bm
  Right now, you think that she's perfection.

A
  This time is really an exception.

Bm
  Well, you know I hate to be a downer,

A
  But I'm the guy she left before you found her.

   D A/C♯ Bm A
Well, I'm not   say - ing

    G♯m7♭5   C♯7   F♯m   A7/E
You ___won't have a good love with her.

   D A/C♯ Bm A G♯m7♭5
But I keep on re - memberin'

    C♯7   F♯m
Things ___ like they were.

Pre-Chorus 2

        C♯7
She made me feel so bad,

        F♯m
She made my heart feel sad.

        C♯7
She made my days go wrong,

        C♯m7
And made my nights so long.

        E7
You got to keep in mind...

Chorus 2   *Repeat Chorus 1*

Interlude

```
‖: Bm*   A*  Bm* |            | A*    E*  A* |          :‖
 | D  A/C♯ Bm A | G♯m7♭5 C♯7 | F♯m         | A7/E      |
 | D  A/C♯ Bm A | G♯m7♭5 C♯7 | F♯m         | C♯7       |
 | F♯m          | C♯7        | C♯m7        | E7        |
```
                                       Keep in mind...

Outro   *Repeat Chorus 1 till fade*

Heroes and Villains

Words and Music by
Brian Wilson and Van Dyke Parks

Melody:

I've been in this town _ so long that

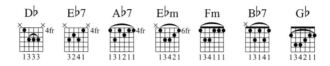

Db   Eb7   Ab7   Ebm   Fm   Bb7   Gb

Verse 1

                Db
I've been in this town

So long that back in the city

I've been taken for a lost and gone
                          Eb7
And unknown for a long, ____ long time.

      Ab7
Fell in love years ago with an innocent girl

Who from the Spanish and Indian home
                       Db
Full of the heroes and villains.

Verse 2

          Db
Once at night Catillion squared the fight

And she was right in the rain
                    Eb7
Of the bullets that eventually brought her down.

      Ab7
But she's still dancing in the night

Unafraid of what a dude'll do
                   Db   **N.C.**
In a town full of heroes and villians.

Copyright © 1967 IRVING MUSIC, INC.
Copyright Renewed
All Rights Reserved   Used by Permission

Chorus

E♭m
Heroes and villains,

              A♭7
Just see what you've done, done.

E♭m
Heroes and villains,

              A♭7
Just see what you done, done.

Fm   **B♭7**
Na, na, na, na, na,

E♭m   **G♭**
Na, na, na, na.

Verse 3

D♭
La, la, la, la, la, la, la, la.

La, la, la, la, la, la, la, la.

           E♭7
La, la, la, la, la, la, la, la.

      A♭7
Stand or fall, I know there shall be

Peace in the valley,

And it's all an affair of my

         D♭7
Life with the heroes and villains.

Interlude 1 | **N.C.** | | | | | |

　　　　　　　　　　| | | | | | |

Bridge

N.C.
My children were raised,

You know they suddenly rise.

They started slow long ago,

Head to toe, healthy, wealthy and wise.

Interlude 2

N.C.
I've been in this town

So long, so long to the city,

I'm fit with the stuff

To ride in the rough,

And sunny down snuff,

I'm alright by the heroes and...

Outro

E♭m
‖: Heroes and villains,

　　　　　　　　　　A♭7
Just see what you've done, done. :‖ ***Repeat and fade***

I Get Around

Words and Music by
Brian Wilson and Mike Love

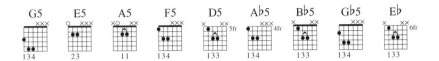

Intro

N.C.
(Round, round, get around.

I get around, yeah.

Get around, round, round,

I get around.)

Chorus 1

      G5   **E5**
I get a-round from town to town.
             A5
I'm a real cool head.
               F5   **D5**
I'm makin' real good bread.

Copyright © 1964 IRVING MUSIC, INC.
Copyright Renewed
All Rights Reserved   Used by Permission

Verse 1

          A5   D5   A5   D5
I'm gettin' bugged drivin' up and down the same old strip.

          A5   D5   A5   D5
I gotta find a new place where the kids are hip.

| N.C. | |

          A5   D5   A5   D5
My buddies and me__ are gettin' real well known,

          A5   D5   A5   D5
Yeah, the bad guys know us and they leave us a-lone.

Chorus 2

          G5   E5
I get a-round from town to town.

                    A5
I'm a real cool head.

                      F5   D5
I'm makin' real good bread.

          E5
(I get a-round.) (Round.) Get around, round, round.

Solo | A | | D | | |
          | A | | E | F | |

THE BEACH BOYS   79

Verse 2

       B♭5   E♭5   B♭5   E♭5
We always take my car 'cause it's never been beat.

         B♭5   E♭5   B♭5   E♭5
And we've never missed yet with the girls we meet.

| N.C. | | |

         B♭5   E♭5   B♭5   E♭5
None of the guys go steady 'cause it wouldn't be right,

        B♭5   E♭5   B♭5   E♭5
To leave their best girl home on a Saturday night.

Chorus 3

       A♭5   F5
I get a-round from town to town.

               B♭5
I'm a real cool head.

                   G♭5   E♭5
I'm makin' real good bread.

     F5   E♭5
(I get a-round.) (Round.) Oo.

Outro

   A♭5 N.C.
(Round, round, get around.

I get around, yeah.

Get around, round, round,

I get around.)

      A♭5   F5
‖: I get a-round from town to town.

              B♭5
I'm a real cool head.

               G♭5   E♭5
I'm makin' real good bread.   :‖ *Repeat and fade*

I Just Wasn't Made for These Times

Words and Music by
Brian Wilson and Tony Asher

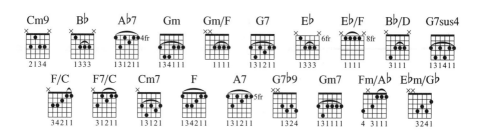

Verse 1

  Cm9   **Bb**
I keep lookin' for a place to fit in

    Ab7   **Gm Gm/F**
Where I can speak my mind.

  Cm9   **Bb**
And I've been tryin' hard to find the people

    Ab7   **Gm G7**
That I won't leave behind.

  Eb   **Eb/F**
They say I got brains,

     Bb/D   **Gm**   **G7sus4**
But they ain't doin' me no good;

            G7
I wish they could.

Copyright © 1966 IRVING MUSIC, INC.
Copyright Renewed
All Rights Reserved   Used by Permission

Pre-Chorus 1

| Cm9 | F/C | | Cm9 | F/C |

Each time things start to happen again,

| Cm9 | F/C | | Cm9 | F/C |

I think I got somethin' good goin' for myself,

F7/C

But what goes wrong?

Chorus 1

Cm7   F

Sometimes I feel very sad.

Cm7   F

Sometimes I feel very sad.

Cm7   F

Sometimes I feel very sad

| E♭ | A7 | G7sus4 | G7♭9 |

| Cm9 | F/C | Cm9 | E♭/F | Cm9 | B♭ | Gm7 |

I guess I just wasn't made for these times.

Verse 2

Cm9   B♭

Ev'ry time I get the inspiration

A♭7   Gm Gm/F

To go change things around,

Cm9   B♭

No one wants to help me look for places

A♭7   Gm G7

Where new things might be found.

E♭   E♭/F

Where can I turn

B♭/D   Gm   G7sus4

When my fair weather friends cop out?

G7

What's it all about?

Pre-Chorus 2   *Repeat Pre-Chorus 1*

Chorus 2

Cm7   F
Sometimes I feel very sad.

Cm7   F
Can't find nothin' I can put my heart and soul into.

Cm7   F
Can't find nothin' I can put my heart and soul into.

| Eb   A7 | G7sus4 G7b9 |

Cm9 F/C Cm9   Eb/F
I guess I just wasn't made for these times.

Interlude

| N.C. | | Cm9 | Bb |
| Ab7 | G7sus4 G7b9 |

Outro

  Cm9 F/C Cm9   F/C
||: I guess I just wasn't made for these times.

Cm9 F/C Cm9   F/C
I guess I just wasn't made for these times.

Cm9 F/C Fm/Ab   G7
I guess I just wasn't made for these...

Ebm/Gb   Eb/F
I guess I just wasn't made for these times. :|| *Repeat and fade*

In My Room

Words and Music by
Brian Wilson and Gary Usher

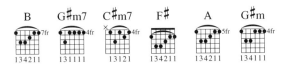

B   G#m7   C#m7   F#   A   G#m

Intro

| B   G#m7 | C#m7   F# | |

Verse 1

B
There's a world where I can go and

      A   B   G#m7
Tell my secrets to.

      C#m7   A   F#
In my room,

      B   A   B
In my room. (In my room.)

Verse 2

B
In this world I lock out all my

      A   B   G#m7
Worries and my fears.

      C#m7   A   F#
In my room,

      B   A   B
In my room. (In my room.)

Copyright © 1964 IRVING MUSIC, INC.
Copyright Renewed
All Rights Reserved   Used by Permission

Bridge

G♯m   F♯
Do my dreaming, and my scheming,

G♯m F♯ G♯m F♯ B
Lie   a - wake and pray.

G♯m   F♯
Do my crying and my sighing,

C♯m7   F♯
Laugh at yesterday.

Verse 3

B
Now it's dark and I'm alone but

      A   B   G♯m7
I won't be a-fraid

      C♯m7   A   F♯
In my room,

      B
In my room.

Outro

    A   B   A   B
‖: In my room, in my room. :‖   *Repeat and fade*

It's OK

Words and Music by
Brian Wilson and Mike Love

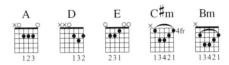

Verse 1

       A
Fun is in, it's no sin, it's that time again

       D
To shed your load, hit the road, on the run again.

       A
Summer skies in our eyes and a warmer sun.

       D
It's one for all, all for one, all for all out fun.

Chorus 1

E   C#m   D Bm
Got - ta go to it.

E   C#m   D   Bm
Gon - na go through it.

E   C#m   D   Bm
Got - ta get with it.

Copyright © 1976 Brother Publishing Company (BMI)
All Rights Reserved   Used by Permission

Verse 2

     A
Lookin' good down the hood of a funky ride

     D
On the way to the tide just to tan your hide.

     A
In the shade, lemonade, in the sun ocean spray,

       D
To get your face in the race or lay back's no disgrace.

Chorus 2   *Repeat Chorus 1*

Verse 3

     A
It's O-K to get out there and have some fun

     D
By your-self maybe or else with a special one.

     A
Good or bad, glad or sad, it's all gonna pass,

     D
So it's O-K, let's all play and enjoy while it lasts.

Chorus 3   *Repeat Chorus 1*

Outro

     A
Find a ride,

     D
Find a ride.

     A
‖: Find a ride,

     D
Find a ride.   :‖ ***Repeat and fade***

Keep an Eye on Summer

Words and Music by
Brian Wilson and Bob Norberg

Melody:

Keep an eye on sum - mer.

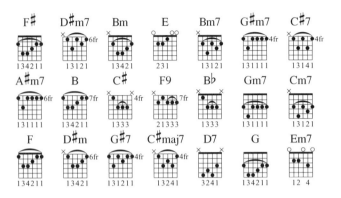

Intro

F#	D#m7 Bm E

Keep an eye on sum-mer.

F#	D#m7 Bm7 E

Keep an eye on sum-mer.

Verse 1

F#	D#m7	G#m7 C#7

We said good-bye last Sep-tember.

F#	D#m7	G#m7 C#7

Your words I still can hear.

F#	A#m7

Keep an eye on

B	G#m7 C# F# D#m7 Bm7 E

Summer   this year.

© 1964 (Renewed 1992) SCREEN GEMS-EMI MUSIC INC.
All Rights Reserved   International Copyright Secured   Used by Permission

Verse 2

F♯   D♯m7 G♯m7 C♯7
Those things I say in my letters,

F♯   D♯m7 G♯m7 C♯7
You'll find they're all sin - cere.

F♯ A♯m7
Keep an eye on

B G♯m7 C♯ F♯ Bm F♯ F9
Summer   this year.

Bridge

B♭   Gm7 Cm7 F
Soon we'll be gradu - ating

B♭   Gm7 Cm7 F
And we'll be so far a-part.

C♯   A♯m7 D♯m G♯7
And though you could be dating,

 C♯ C♯maj7 C♯7
I'm waiting _____ and waiting.

Verse 3

F♯   D♯m7 G♯m7 C♯7
And as we look at the future,

F♯   D♯m7 G♯m7 C♯7
Though it be through a tear,

F♯ A♯m7 B G♯m7 C♯7 D7
Keep an eye on summer _____ this

Outro

‖: G Em7 | Cm7 F :‖ *Repeat and fade*
year.

Kokomo

from the Motion Picture COCKTAIL
Words and Music by Mike Love, Terry Melcher,
John Phillips and Scott McKenzie

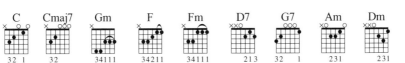

Intro

N.C.

(Aruba, Jamaica,

Ooh, I wanna take ya.

Bermuda, Bahama,

Come on, pretty mama.

Key Largo, Montego,

Baby, why don't we go, Jamaica?)

Verse 1

                         C   Cmaj7

Off the Florida Keys

Gm   F

    There's a place called Kokomo.

Fm   C

    That's where you wanna go

             D7   G7

To get a-way from it all.

C   Cmaj7

    Bodies in the sand,

Gm   F

    Tropical drink melting in your hand.

© 1988 Touchstone Pictures Music & Songs, Inc., Buena Vista Music Company, Clair Audient Publishing,
Daywin Music, Inc., Honest John Music and Phillips-Tucker Music
Administered 100% by Touchstone Pictures Music & Songs, Inc. and Buena Vista Music Company

```
Fm                          C
    We'll be falling in love
                  D7
To the rhythm of a steel drum band
G7                    C
    Down in Kokomo.


                 C
Chorus 1    A-ruba, Jamaica,

            Ooh, I wanna take you
                 F
            To Ber-muda, Bahama,

            Come on, pretty mama.
                 C
            Key Largo, Montego,
                                 F
            Baby, why don't we go?
            Ooh, I wanna take you down to Kokomo.
                 Fm                    C
            We'll get there fast and then we'll take it slow.
            Am              Dm        G7
                That's where we wanna go,
                                 C
            Way down in Kokomo.

            La Martinique,

            That Montserrat mystique.


                 C                   Cmaj7
Verse 2          We'll put out to sea
            Gm                      F
                And we'll perfect our chemistry.
            Fm                    C
                By and by we'll defy
```

           D7   **G7**
A little bit of gravity.

C   **Cmaj7**
   Afternoon delight,

Gm   **F**
   Cocktails and moonlit nights.

Fm   **C**
   That dreamy look in your eye,

                D7
Give me a tropical contact high

G7   **C**
   Way down in Kokomo.

           C
Chorus 2   A-ruba, Jamaica,

Ooh, I wanna take you

        F
To Ber-muda, Bahama,

Come on, pretty mama.

      C
Key Largo, Montego,

                      F
Baby, why don't we go?
Ooh, I wanna take you down to Kokomo.

        Fm   **C**
We'll get there fast and then we'll take it slow.

Am   **Dm**   **G7**
   That's where we wanna go,

                C
Way down in Kokomo.

Port Au Prince,

I wanna catch a glimpse.

Solo | C | Cmaj7 | Gm | F | |
| Fm | C | D7 | G7 | |

Verse 3

C   Cmaj7
   Ev'rybody knows

Gm   F
   A little place like Kokomo.

Fm   C
   Now if you wanna go

        D7
And get a-way from it all,

G7   C
   Go down to Kokomo.

Chorus 3

    C
‖: A-ruba, Jamaica,

Ooh, I wanna take you

   F
To Ber-muda, Bahama,

Come on, pretty mama.

   C
Key Largo, Montego,

                       F
Baby, why don't we go?
Ooh, I wanna take you down to Kokomo.

   Fm   C
We'll get there fast and then we'll take it slow.

Am   Dm   G7
   That's where we wanna go,

                  C
Way down in Kokomo.   :‖   *Repeat and fade*

Let Him Run Wild

Words and Music by
Brian Wilson and Mike Love

Melody:

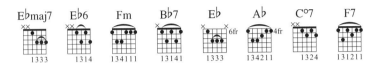

When I watched you walk with him, —

Ebmaj7   Eb6   Fm   Bb7   Eb   Ab   C°7   F7

Intro

| Ebmaj7 | Eb6 | Fm | Bb7 | |

Verse 1

Ebmaj7   Eb6
When I watched you walk with him,

Ebmaj7   Eb6
Tears filled my eyes.

    Ebmaj7   Eb6
And when I heard you talk with him

Fm   Bb7
I couldn't stand his lies.

Fm   Bb7
    And now be-fore he tries it,

Fm   Bb7
    I hope you realize it.

Chorus 1

Eb
Let him run wild, he don't care.

Ab
Let him run wild, he'll find out.

Eb   C°7   F7
Let him run wild, he don't care.

    Fm   Bb7
(Guess you know I waited for you.)

Copyright © 1965 IRVING MUSIC, INC.
Copyright Renewed
All Rights Reserved   Used by Permission

Verse 2

E♭maj7   E♭6
He'll do the same to other girls

E♭maj7   E♭6
That he did to you,

E♭maj7   E♭6
But then one day he'll run into one

Fm   B♭7
That's gonna hurt him too.

Fm   B♭7
Before he makes you over,

Fm   B♭7
I'm gonna take you over.

Chorus 2

Repeat Chorus 1

Verse 3

E♭maj7   E♭6
All the dreams you shared with him

E♭maj7   E♭6
You might as well for-get.

E♭maj7   E♭6
I know you need a truer love,

Fm   B♭7
And that's what you'll get.

Fm   B♭7
And now that you don't need him,

Fm   B♭7
Well, he can have his freedom.

Outro

E♭
‖: Let him run wild, he don't care.

A♭
Let him run wild, he'll find out. :‖   ***Repeat and fade***

Little Deuce Coupe

Music by Brian Wilson
Words by Roger Christian

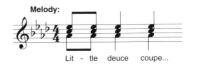

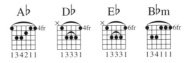

Intro

A♭
Little deuce coupe you don't know,

You don't know what I got.

Verse 1

A♭
Well, I'm not braggin' babe, so don't put me down,

But I've got the fastest set of wheels in town.

D♭
When somethin' comes up to me, he don't even try,

A♭
'Cause if it had a set of wings, man I know she could fly.

Chorus 1

E♭   **B♭m**
She's my little deuce coupe.

E♭   **B♭m**   **A♭**
  You don't know__ what I got.

Verse 2

A♭
Just a little deuce coupe with a flat head mill,

But she'll walk a Thunderbird like she's standin' still.

D♭
She's ported and relieved and she's stroked and bored.

A♭
She'll do a hundred and forty in the top end floored.

Copyright © 1963 by Careers-BMG Music Publishing, Inc. and Irving Music, Inc.
Copyright Renewed
International Copyright Secured   All Rights Reserved

Chorus 2   *Repeat Chorus 1*

                D♭

Bridge   She's got a competition clutch with a four on the floor

           A♭

And she purrs like a kitten till the lake pipes roar.

        D♭

And if that ain't enough to make you flip your lid,

       B♭m   **E♭ N.C.**

There's one more thing, I got the pink slip, daddy.

      A♭

Verse 3   And comin' off the line when the light turns green,

Well, she blows 'em out of the water like you never seen.

      D♭

I get pushed out of shape, and it's hard to steer

       A♭

When I get rubber in all four gears.

Chorus 3   *Repeat Chorus 1*

Outro   *Repeat Chorus 1 till fade*

The Little Girl I Once Knew

Words and Music by Brian Wilson

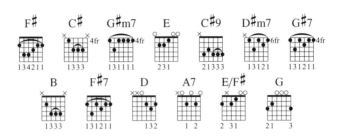

Intro   ‖: F♯ | C♯ | G♯m7 | E :‖

Verse 1

    G♯m7   C♯9
    We met when she was younger,

    G♯m7   C♯9
    Then I had no eyes for her.

    D♯m7   G♯7
    A few years went by and I saw her;

    D♯m7   G♯7
    Now I'm gonna try for her.

    C♯   F♯ N.C.
    Look out, babe.

Chorus 1

    B   F♯7   B
    She's not the little girl I once knew.

                 E
She's not the little girl I once...

    D   A7   D
    She's not the little girl I once knew.

         E/F♯   G♯m7
She's not the little girl I once knew.

Copyright © 1965 IRVING MUSIC, INC.
Copyright Renewed
All Rights Reserved   Used by Permission

Verse 2

G♯m7   C♯9
How could I ever have known that

G♯m7   C♯9
  She'd be what she is today?

D♯m7   G♯7
  Look at how her boyfriend holds her;

D♯m7   G♯7
  I'll be moving in one day.

C♯   F♯ N.C.
  Split, man.

Chorus 2

B   F♯7   B
  She's not the little girl I once knew.

           E   D
She's not the little girl I once knew.

          A7   D
She's not the little girl I once knew.

         E/F♯   B
She's not the little girl I once knew.

Interlude | B | | E | | B | |

Bridge

E
La, doo, day, a pow, pow, pow.

B
La, doo, day, a pow, pow, pow.

E
La, doo, day, a pow, pow, pow.

Chorus 3

D   A7   D
 She's not the little girl I once knew.

     G   D
She's not the little girl I once knew.

     A7   D
She's not the little girl I once knew.

      E/F♯   B C♯ G♯m7 E
She's not the little girl I once knew.

| B | C♯ | G♯m7 | E | |

Outro

   B   F♯7   B
‖: She's not the little girl I once knew.

      E   B
She's not the little girl I once knew. :‖ *Repeat and fade*

Salt Lake City

Words and Music by
Brian Wilson and Mike Love

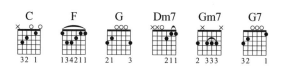

Verse 1

      C   **F**   **C**
Down in Utah the guys and I __ dig a city called Salt Lake.

                           F   **C**
It's got the grooviest kids, that's why we never get tired of Salt Lake.

     G   **Dm7**   **Gm7**   **C**
And the way the kids talk so cool __ is an out-of-sight thing.

      F   **G**
And the Number One radio station makes the town really swing.

Dm7   **G7**   **C**
Salt Lake City, we'll be comin' soon.

Verse 2

       C   **F**   **C**
There's a park near the city, yeah, __ all the kids dig the La-goon, now.

                             F   **C**
It's full of all kinds of girls, and rides, and we'll be flyin' there soon, now.

     G   **Dm7**   **Gm7**   **C**
And girl for girl they've got the cut - est of the Western states.

      F   **G**
They got the sun in the summer, and wintertime the skiing is great.

Dm7   **G7**   **C**
Salt Lake City, we'll be comin' soon.

Copyright © 1965 IRVING MUSIC, INC.
Copyright Renewed
All Rights Reserved   Used by Permission

Little Honda

Words and Music by
Brian Wilson and Mike Love

Melody:

I'm gon-na wake you up ear-ly 'cause I'm

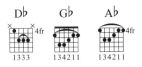

Db   Gb   Ab

Intro

| **Db** | | |

Go!

Verse 1

        Db
I'm gonna wake you up early

'Cause I'm gonna take a ride with you.

    Gb
We're going down to the Honda shop,

         Db
I'll tell you what we're gonna do.

   Ab
Put on a ragged sweatshirt,

            Db   **Ab**
I'll take you anywhere you want me to.

Chorus 1

   Db   **Gb**
First gear, it's all right.

      Db   **Gb**
Second gear, __ a lean right.

     Db   **Gb**
Third gear, __ hang on tight.

  Ab
(Faster. It's all right.)

Copyright © 1964 IRVING MUSIC, INC.
Copyright Renewed
All Rights Reserved   Used by Permission

Verse 2

$D\flat$
It's not a big motorcycle,

Just a groovy little motorbike.

$G\flat$
It's more fun than a barrel of monkeys,

$D\flat$
That two-wheeled bike.

$A\flat$
We'll ride on out of the town

$D\flat$ $A\flat$
To anyplace I know you like.

Chorus 2   *Repeat Chorus 1*

Verse 3

$D\flat$
It climbs the hills like a Matchless

'Cause my Honda's built really light.

$G\flat$
When I go into the turns,

$D\flat$
Tilt with me and hang on tight.

$A\flat$
I'd better turn on the lights

$D\flat$ $A\flat$
So we can ride my Honda tonight.

Chorus 3   *Repeat Chorus 1*

Outro   *Repeat Chorus 1 and fade*

Little Saint Nick

Words and Music by
Brian Wilson and Mike Love

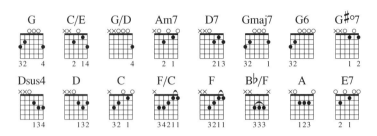

Intro | G   C/E   G/D   C/E | G   C/E   G/D   C/E |

Am7
Ooh.

D7   **G**
Merry Christmas, Saint Nick.
          (Christmas comes this time each year.)

Am7   **D7**
Ooh.

Verse 1
          Am7   **D7**   **Am7**   **D7**
Well, way up north where the air gets cold,

          G   **Gmaj7**   **G6**   **G♯°7**
There's a tale about Christmas that you've all been told.

          Am7   **D7**   **Am7**   **D7**
And a real famous cat all dressed up in red,

          G   **Gmaj7**   **G6**
And he spends his whole year workin' out on his sled.

Chorus 1
          C
It's the little Saint Nick. (Little Saint Nick.)

          Am7   **Dsus4 D**
It's the little Saint Nick. (Little Saint   Nick.)

Copyright © 1963 IRVING MUSIC, INC.
Copyright Renewed

Verse 2

    Am7   D7   Am7   D7
Just a little bob-sled, we call it Old Saint Nick,

     G   Gmaj7   G6   G♯°7
And she'll walk a to-boggan with a four-speed stick.

      Am7   D7   Am7   D7
She's a candy-apple red with a ski for a wheel,

     G   Gmaj7   G6
And when Santa gives her gas, man, just watch her peel.

Chorus 2   *Repeat Chorus 1*

Bridge

C   F/C   C
Run, run, rein - deer.

F   B♭/F   F
Run, run, rein - deer.

   C   F/C   C
Oh, run, run, rein - deer.

A
Run, run, reindeer.

     N.C.
He don't miss no one.

Verse 3

    Am7   D7   Am7   D7
And haulin' through the snow at a fright'nin' speed

     G   Gmaj7   G6   G♯°7
With a half a dozen deer with Rudy to lead.

    Am7   D7   Am7   D7
He's gotta wear his goggles 'cause the snow really flies,

     G   Gmaj7   G6   G7
And he's cruisin' ev'ry pad with a little surprise.

Chorus 3   *Repeat Chorus 1*

Please Let Me Wonder

Words and Music by
Brian Wilson and Mike Love

Melody:

Now, _ here we are to-geth - er,

Chords
F · Gm · C · F7 · Bb · Dm · A7 · Dm(maj7) · Dm7 · Am · Gm7/C · F9 · D7 · Gm7 · C9 · Fmaj7 · Gm/F · Dm/G · G · Eb/F

Intro

‖: F | | Gm | C :‖

Verse 1

F   F7
Now, here we are together,

Bb   C
This would've been worth waiting forever;

F   Dm   Gm C
I always knew it'd feel this way.

F   F7
And please for - give my shaking.

Bb   Gm   A7
Can't you tell my heart is breaking?

Dm   Dm(maj7) Dm7
Can't make myself say

      Am   Bb Gm7/C
What I planned to say, baby.

Chorus 1

      F9
(Please let me wonder.)

      D7
(Please let me wonder.)

Gm7   C9   Fmaj7   Gm/F
(Please let me wonder, love.)

Copyright © 1965 IRVING MUSIC, INC.
Copyright Renewed
All Rights Reserved   Used by Permission

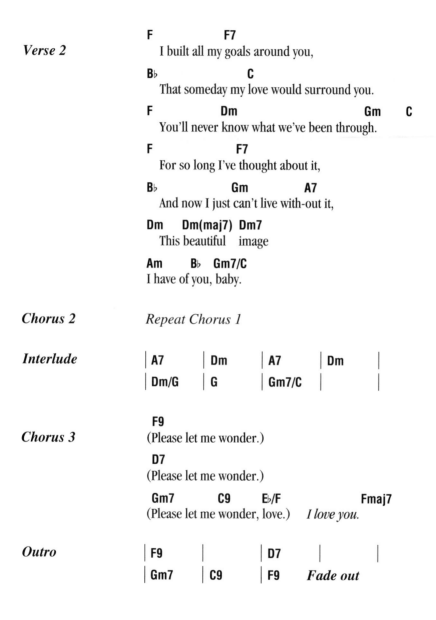

Verse 2

    F   F7
I built all my goals around you,

    B♭   C
That someday my love would surround you.

    F   Dm   Gm   C
You'll never know what we've been through.

    F   F7
For so long I've thought about it,

    B♭   Gm   A7
And now I just can't live with-out it,

    Dm   Dm(maj7) Dm7
This beautiful   image

    Am   B♭   Gm7/C
I have of you, baby.

Chorus 2   *Repeat Chorus 1*

Interlude

| A7 | Dm | A7 | Dm | |
| Dm/G | G | Gm7/C | | |

Chorus 3

F9
(Please let me wonder.)

D7
(Please let me wonder.)

Gm7   C9   E♭/F   Fmaj7
(Please let me wonder, love.) *I love you.*

Outro

| F9 | | D7 | | |
| Gm7 | C9 | F9 | *Fade out* | |

Shut Down

Words by Roger Christian
Music by Brian Wilson

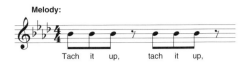

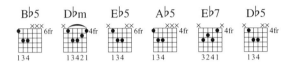

Intro

B♭5
Tach it up, tach it up,

D♭m   **E♭5**   **A♭5**   **E♭7**
Buddy, gonna shut you down.

Verse 1

A♭5
It happened on the strip where the road is wide,

Two cool shorts standin' side by side.

D♭5
Yeah, my fuel-injected Stingray and a four-thirteen

A♭5
A revvin' up their engines and it sounds real mean.

B♭5
Tach it up, tach it up,

D♭5   **E♭5**   **A♭5**   **E♭7**
Buddy, gonna shut you down.

Copyright © 1963 IRVING MUSIC, INC.
Copyright Renewed and Assigned to IRVING MUSIC, INC. and
CAREERS-BMG MUSIC PUBLISHING, INC. for the USA
All Rights Reserved   Used by Permission

Verse 2

A♭5
Declining numbers at an even rate.

At the count of one we both accelerate.

D♭5
My Stingray is light, the slicks are startin' to spin,

A♭5
But the four-thirteen's really diggin' in.

B♭5   **D♭5**   **E♭5**   **A♭5**
Gotta be cool now, power shift here we go.

Bridge

D♭5
The super stock Dodge is winding out in low

A♭5
But my fuel injected Stingray's really startin' to go.

D♭5
To get the traction, I'm riding the clutch.

A♭5   **E♭7**
My pressure plate is burnin' and the sheen's too much.

Guitar Solo

| **D♭5** | | | **A♭5** | | |
| **D♭5** | | | **A♭5** | | **E♭7** | |

Verse 3

A♭5
Pedals to the floor, hear his dual quads drinkin',

Now the four-thirteen's lead is startin' to shrink.

D♭5
He's hot with ram induction but it's understood,

A♭5
I gotta fuel injected engine sittin' under my hood.

Outro

B♭5
‖: Shut it off, shut it off,

D♭5   **E♭5**   **A♭5**
Buddy, now I shut you down.   :‖ *Repeat and fade*

Sloop John B

Words and Music by Brian Wilson

We come on the sloop, John _ B.,

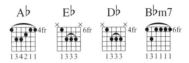

Verse 1

          A♭
We come on the sloop, John B.,

My grandfather and me.

                          E♭
Around Nassau town we did roam.

              A♭
Drinking all night,

          D♭   **B♭m7**
Got into a fight.

            A♭
Well, I feel so broke up,

E♭   **A♭**
   I wanna go home.

Copyright © 1966 New Executive Music
Copyright Renewed
International Copyright Secured All Rights Reserved

Chorus 1

      A♭
So hoist up the John B. sail.

See how the mainsail sets.

                                   E♭
Call for the captain ashore, let me go home.

       A♭
Let me go home.

             D♭   **B♭m7**
I wanna go home, a yeah, yeah.

       A♭
Well, I feel so broke up,

E♭   **A♭**
  I wanna go home.

Verse 2

      A♭
The first mate, he got drunk,

Broke in the captain's trunk.

                                   E♭
The constable had to come and take him a-way.

        A♭
Sheriff John Stone,

               D♭   **B♭m7**
Why don't you leave me a-lone? A yeah, yeah.

       A♭
Well, I feel so broke up

E♭   **A♭**
  I wanna go home.

Chorus 2   A♭
So hoist up the John B. sail.

See how the mainsail sets.

                  E♭
Call for the captain ashore, let me go home,

Let me go home.

I wanna go home. Let me go...

Why don't you let me go home?

     A♭
Well, I feel so broke up

E♭   A♭
  I wanna go home.

     A♭
Verse 3   The poor cook, he caught the fits

And threw away all my grits

                  E♭
And then he took and he ate up all of my corn.

      A♭
Let me go home.

            D♭   B♭m7
Why don't they let me go home?

      A♭
This is ___ the worst trip

E♭   A♭
  I've ever been on.

Outro   *Repeat Chorus 2 and fade*

Spirit of America

Words and Music by
Brian Wilson and Roger Christian

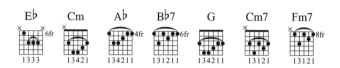

Eb	Cm	Ab	Bb7	G	Cm7	Fm7
1333	13421	134211	131211	134211	13121	13121

Intro

| Eb | Cm | |

Ab   **Bb7**
Spirit of A-merica.

Eb   **Cm**
Spirit of A-merica,

Ab   **Bb7**
Spirit of A-merica.

Verse 1

      Eb   **Cm**
The Bonneville Salt Flats

    Ab   **Bb7**
Had seen some strange things,

    Eb   **Cm**
But the strangest thing yet

    Ab   **Bb7**
Was a jet without wings.

G
Once as a jet it played in the stars,

    Cm   **Cm7**
But now on the ground

    Fm7   **Bb7**
It's the king of all cars.

Copyright © 1963, 1964 IRVING MUSIC, INC. and CAREERS-BMG MUSIC PUBLISHING, INC. for the USA
Copyright Renewed
All Rights outside the USA Controlled by IRVING MUSIC, INC.
All Rights Reserved   Used by Permission

Chorus 1

Eb   Cm
Spirit of A-merica,

Ab   Bb7
Spirit of A-merica.

Eb   Cm
Spirit of A-merica,

Ab   Bb7
Spirit of A-merica.

Verse 2

     Eb   Cm
An airplane, an auto,

      Ab   Bb7
Now famous world-wide.

      Eb   Cm
The Spirit of A-merica,

     Ab   Bb7
The name on the side.

     G
The man who would drive her,

Craig Breedlove by name,

 Cm   Cm7
A daring young man

      Fm7   Bb7
Played a dangerous game.

Chorus 2   *Repeat Chorus 1*

Verse 3

      E♭   **Cm**
With a J-forty-seven,

  A♭   **B♭7**
A jet for his power,

      E♭   **Cm**
Craig Breedlove had averaged

    A♭   **B♭7**
Four-o-seven per hour.

    G
Both man and machine

Had given fair warn.

     Cm   **Cm7**
They'd set a new record

      Fm7   **B♭7**
On that warm August morn.

Outro   *Repeat Chorus 1 and fade*

Surf's Up

Words and Music by
Brian Wilson and Van Dyke Parks

Melody:

A dia - mond neck-lace played _ the pawn,

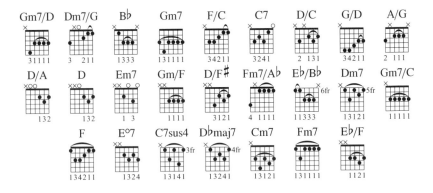

Verse 1

Gm7/D
A diamond necklace played the pawn,

Hand and hand some drummed along,

Dm7/G
Oh, ____ to a handsome man and baton.

Gm7/D
A blind class aristocracy,

Back through the opera glass

Dm7/G
You see ____ the pit and the pendulum drawn.

Bb   **Gm7**   **F/C C7 D/C**
Column - ated ruins dom - i - no.

G/D   **A/G**
Canvass the town and brush the backdrop.

D/A
Are you sleeping?

Copyright © 1971 (Renewed 1999) Brother Publishing Company (BMI)
All Rights Reserved   Used by Permission

Verse 2

Gm7/D
   Hung velvet overtaken me,

Dim chandelier awaken me
Dm7/G
   To a song dissolved in the dawn.
Gm7/D
   The music hall a costly bow.

The music all is lost for now
Dm7/G
   To a muted trumpeter swan.

B♭   **Gm7**   **F/C** **C7** **D/C**
Column-ated ruins dom - i - no.
G/D   **A/G**
Canvass the town and brush the backdrop.

        D/A   **D** **Em7** **Gm/F** **D/F♯**
Are you sleeping, Brother John?

Verse 3

Fm7/A♭
   Dove nested towers the hour was
E♭/B♭
Strike the street, quicksilver moon.
Fm7/A♭
   Carriage across the fog,
   E♭/B♭
Two step to lamplights cellar tune.
   Dm7   **Gm7/C** **C7** **F**
The laughs come hard in Auld   Lang Syne.

Bridge

Dm7
The glass was raised, the fired rose,

  F/C   **C7**
The fullness of the wine.

      E°7 **F**
The dim last toast - ing

Dm7   **Gm7/C C7** **F**
While at port a - dieu   or die.

  Dm7
A choke of grief hard hardened I

   Gm7/C   **C7sus4 C7**   **F**
Be - yond be - lief a   broken man too tough to cry.

Verse 4

Fm7/A♭
  Surfs up, mm, mm, mm, mm, mm,

E♭/B♭
Mm, aboard a tidal wave.

Fm7/A♭
  Come about hard and join

  E♭/B♭
The young and often spring you gave.

  D♭maj7   **Cm7**
I heard the word, won-derful thing,

  Fm7   **E♭/F** **B♭** **Cm7**
A children's song.

Outro

Fm7
Child, child, child,

  Cm7
Is the father of the man.

B♭
Child, child, child,

  Cm7
Is the father of the man.

 Fm7   **Cm7**
A children's song,

    B♭   **Cm7**
Have you listened as they ___ played?

    Fm7 **Cm7**
They're song is love,

    B♭   **Cm7**
And the children know the ___ way.

    Fm7 **Cm7**
‖: Na, na, na, na.

    B♭   **Cm7**
Na, na, na, na, na, na, na.   :‖ *Repeat and fade*

Surfer's Rule

Words and Music by
Brian Wilson and Mike Love

Melody:

It's plas-tered on the wall

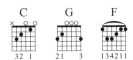

C   G   F
32 1 21 3 134211

Verse 1

          C
It's plastered on the wall all around the school, now,

                                          G
Becoming just as common as the Golden Rule, now.

C   F
Take it or leave it,

            C   F
But you better be-lieve it,

            C
Surfer's rule.

Copyright © 1963 IRVING MUSIC, INC.
Copyright Renewed
All Rights Reserved   Used by Permission

Verse 2
    C
They burn it on the grass on the football field, now;

                                              G
Just try to make them cool it and they'll never yield, now.

C   **F**
Take what you've heard, now,

    C   **F**
And go pass the word, now,

      C
Surfer's rule.

                            G
It's a genuine fact that the surfer's rule.

Verse 3
    C
A woodie full of surfers pulling 'longside the wagon,

                                        G
The hoedaddies sittin' while the surfers are draggin'.

    C   **F**
The surfers are winning,

      C   **F**
And they say as they're winning,

      C
Surfer's rule.

Outro
        F
‖: Surfer's rule.
          (Four seasons, you better believe it.)

      C
Surfer's rule.
          (Four seasons, you better believe it.) :‖ *Repeat and fade*

Surfin' U.S.A.

Words and Music by Chuck Berry

Melody:

If ev -'ry-bod -y had an o - cean...

(Capo 1st fret)

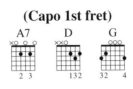

A7   D   G

Verse 1

| N.C. | A7 | N.C. | D |
If everybody had an ocean   across the U.S.A.

| N.C. | A7 | N.C. | D |
Then ev'rybody'd be surfin',   like California.

| N.C. | G |
You'd see them wearin' their bag - gies,

| N.C. | D |
Huarachi sandals too.

| N.C. | A7 |
A bushy, bushy blond hairdo,

| G N.C. | D |
Surfin' U.S.A.

              A7   D
You'll catch 'em surfin' at Del Mar, Ventura County Line,

          A7   D
Santa Cruz and Tressels, Australia's Narabine,

         G   D
All over Man-hattan and down Doheny way.

         A7   G N.C.   D
Ev'rybody's gone surfin',   surfin' U.S.A.

Copyright © 1958, 1963 (Renewed) by Arc Music Corporation (BMI) and Isalee Music Inc. (BMI)
International Copyright Secured All Rights Reserved
Used by Permission

Verse 2

N.C.   A7
We'll all be plannin' out a route

N.C.   D
We're gonna take real soon,

N.C.   A7
We're waxing down our surf boards,

N.C.   D
We can't wait for June.

N.C.   G
We'll all be gone for the sum - mer,

N.C.   D
We're on safari to stay.

N.C.   A7
Tell the teacher we're surfin',

G N.C.   D
Surfin' U.S.A.

                   A7   D
At Haggarty's and Swami's, Pacific Palisades,

                   A7   D
San Onofre and Sunset Redondo Beach, L.A.

                  G   D
All over La Jol - la, and at Waiamea Bay.

                  A7
Ev'rybody's gone surfin',

G N.C.   D
Surfin' U.S.A.

Outro

                  A7
‖: Ev'rybody's gone surfin',

G N.C.   D
Surfin' U.S.A.   :‖   *Repeat and fade*

That's Not Me

Words and Music by
Brian Wilson and Tony Asher

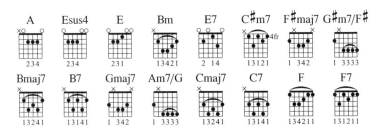

Verse 1

       A
I had to prove that I could make it alone, now,

    Esus4   **E**
But that's not me.

      A
I wanted to show how independent I'd grown, now,

    Esus4   **E**
But that's not me.

      Bm   **E7**
I could try to be big in the eyes of the world.

      Bm
What matters to me

        E7   **C#m7**   **F#maj7**   **G#m7/F#**
Is what I ___ could be to just ___ one girl.

      F#maj7
I'm a little bit scared

      G#m7/F#   **F#maj7**   **G#m7/F#**
'Cause I haven't been home in a long ___ time.

     Bmaj7
You needed my love

        B7   **E7**
And I know ___ that I left at the wrong ___ time.

Copyright © 1966 IRVING MUSIC, INC.
Copyright Renewed
All Rights Reserved   Used by Permission

GUITAR CHORD SONGBOOK

Verse 2

     A
My folks, when I wrote

And told them what I was up to,

  Esus4   **E**
Said that's not me.

     A
I went through all kinds of changes,

Took a look at myself,

   Esus4   **E**
And said, that's not me.

 Bm   **E7**
I missed my pal in the plac - es I've known,

  Bm   **E7**   **G♯m7** **F♯maj7** **G♯m7/F♯**
And ev'ry night as I lay __ there alone I would dream.

 F♯maj7
I once had a dream,

  G♯m7/F♯   **F♯maj7** **G♯m7/F♯**
So I packed up and split for the city.

 Gmaj7
I soon found out

   Am7/G   **Gmaj7** **Am7/G**
That my lonely life wasn't so pretty.

  Cmaj7
I'm glad I went.

    C7   **F**
Now I'm that __ much more sure that we're ready.

F7
Ah, ah, ah.

Outro

    F♯maj7
‖: I once had a dream,

 G♯m7/F♯   **F♯maj7** **G♯m7/F♯**
So I packed up and split for the city.

  F♯maj7
I soon found out

   G♯m7/F♯   **F♯maj7** **G♯m7/F♯**
That my lonely life wasn't so pretty.   :‖ *Repeat and fade*

The Warmth of the Sun

Words and Music by
Brian Wilson and Mike Love

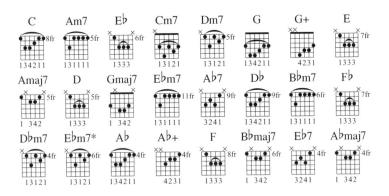

Intro

| C   Am7 | E♭   Cm7 | Dm7 | G   G+ |

Verse 1

       C   Am7
What good is the dawn

E♭   Cm7   Dm7   G   G+
   That grows into day,

       C   Am7
The sunset at night

E♭ Cm7   Dm7   G
   Or living this way?

       E   Amaj7   Am7
For I have the warmth of the sun

       D   Gmaj7   G   G+
With-in me at night.

Copyright © 1964 IRVING MUSIC, INC.
Copyright Renewed
All Rights Reserved   Used by Permission

Verse 2

     C   **Am7**
The love of my life,

Eb   **Cm7**   **Dm7**   **G**   **G+**
   She left me one day.

   C   **Am7**
I cried when she said,

 Eb   **Cm7**   **Dm7**   **G**
   "I don't feel the same way."

    E   **Amaj7**   **Am7**
Still I have the warmth of the sun

    D   **Gmaj7**   **G** **Ebm7** **Ab7**
With-in me to-night.

Verse 3

    Db   **Bbm7**
I'll dream of her arms,

Fb   **Dbm7**   **Ebm7***   **Ab** **Ab+**
   And though they're not real,

   Db   **Bbm7**
Just like she's still there,

Fb   **Dbm7**   **Ebm7***   **Ab**
   The way that I feel.

    F   **Bbmaj7**   **Bbm7**
My love's like the warmth of the sun,

  Eb7   **Abmaj7** **Ab** **Ab+**
It won't ever die.

Outro

‖:**Db** **Bbm7** | **Fb** **Dbm7** | **Ebm7*** | **Ab** **Ab+** :‖ *Repeat and fade*
Ah.   Oo.

Wendy

Words and Music by
Brian Wilson and Mike Love

Melody:

Wen - dy, ___

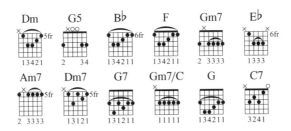

Intro

| Dm | G5 | Dm | B♭ |
| N.C. | F | Gm7 | |

Chorus 1

    F   Gm7
Wendy, Wendy,

                F
What went wrong?

      B♭
Oh, so wrong.

    F   B♭   E♭   Am7
We went to-gether for so long.

Verse 1

Dm7   G7
   I never thought a guy could cry,

Dm7   B♭
   Till you made it with an-other guy.

     F
Oh, Wendy,

Gm7   Gm7/C   F
Wendy left me   alone.

     B♭
Hurts so bad.

Copyright © 1964 IRVING MUSIC, INC.
Copyright Renewed
All Rights Reserved   Used by Permission

Chorus 2

F   Gm7   F

Wendy, Wendy, don't lose your head,

       B♭

Lose your head.

F   B♭   E♭   Am7

Wendy, don't believe a word he said.

Verse 2

Dm7   G7

I can't picture you with him.

Dm7   B♭

His future looks awful dim.

    F

Oh, Wendy,

Gm7   Gm7/C   F   E♭

Wendy left me   alone.

        Dm

Hurts so bad.

Instrumental

Dm	G	Dm	B♭	
F	Dm	Gm7	C7	

Chorus 3	F Gm7 F

Chorus 3

F Gm7   F
Wendy, I wouldn't hurt you like that.

    B♭
No, no, no.

F   B♭   E♭
I thought we had our love down pat.

      Am7
Guess I was wrong.

Verse 3

Dm7   G7
 The farthest thing from my mind,

Dm7   B♭
 Was the day that I'd wake up to find

   F
My Wendy,

Gm7   Gm7/C F
Wendy left me alone.

Interlude | N.C. | F | Gm7 |

Outro

   F
‖: Wendy,

Gm7   F
Wendy left me alone.

     B♭
Hurts so bad. :‖ *Repeat and fade*

When I Grow Up
(To Be a Man)

Words and Music by
Brian Wilson and Mike Love

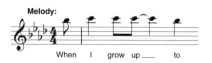

Melody:

When I grow up ___ to

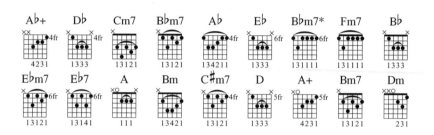

Intro

             A♭+   **D♭** **Cm7** **B♭m7** **A♭**
When I grow up to be ___ a   man.

Verse 1

             A♭
Will I dig the same things

        E♭   **A♭**
That turn me on as a kid?

Will I look back and say

        E♭   **A♭**
That I wish I hadn't done what I did?

           B♭m7* **E♭**
Will I joke a-round

                Cm7   **Fm7**
And still dig those sounds

           A♭+   **D♭** **Cm7** **B♭m7** **A♭** **D♭**
When I grow up to be ___ a   man?

Copyright © 1964 IRVING MUSIC, INC.
Copyright Renewed
All Rights Reserved   Used by Permission

Verse 2

A♭
Will I look for the same things

E♭   **A♭**
In a woman that I dig in a girl?

Will I settle down fast,

    E♭   **A♭**
Or will I first want to travel the world?

              B♭m7* **E♭**
Now I'm young and free,

            Cm7   **Fm7**
But how will it be

    A♭+   **D♭**   **Cm7 B♭m7**
When I grow up to be _____ a

Interlude | **B♭** | | **E♭m7** | **D♭** |
man?

                        | **B♭** | | **E♭m7** | **E♭7** |

Verse 3

        A♭
Will my kids be proud

          E♭   **A♭**
Or think their old man's really a square?

When they're out having fun, yeah,

     E♭   **A♭**
Will I still wanna have my share?

         B♭m7* **E♭**
Will I love my wife

            Cm7   **Fm7**
For the rest of my life

     A♭+   **D♭**   **Cm7 B♭m7 A**
When I grow up to be _____ a   man?

     Bm C♯m D
What will I   be

     A+   **D**   **C♯m7 Bm7 A**
When I grow up to be _____ a   man?

Outro

   A   **Bm**
(Twenty-two, twenty-three.) Won't last for-ever.

         Dm   **A**
(Twenty-four,   twenty-five.) It's kind of sad.

                     Bm
(Twenty-six, twenty-seven.) Won't last for-ever.

         Dm   **A**
(Twenty-eight,   twenty-nine.) It's kind of sad.

                  Bm
(Thirty, thirty-one.) Won't last for-ever.   ***Fade out***

Wind Chimes

Words and Music by Brian Wilson

Hang-ing down from my win - dow, those are my

Dm7/C   G7   C/E   Fadd9   G6   Am7   D7   G7sus2

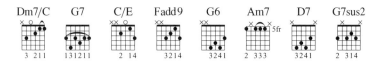

Verse 1

Dm7/C
Hanging down from my window,

G7
Those are my wind chimes.

Dm7/C
On a warm breeze the little bells

G7
Tingle like wind chimes.

C/E   **Fadd9**
Though it's hard

G6   **Am7**   **D7**
I try not to look at my wind chimes.

G7sus2
Now and then a tear rolls off my cheek.

Copyright © 1967 IRVING MUSIC, INC.
Copyright Renewed
All Rights Reserved   Used by Permission

Verse 2

Dm7/C
Close your eyes and lean back now,

      G7
Listen to the wind chimes.

Dm7/C
In the late afternoon

      G7
You're hung up on wind chimes.

C/E   Fadd9
Though it's hard

G6   Am7   D7
I try not to look at my wind chimes.

Outro

G7
(Ba, ba, ba,

Ba, ba, ba, ba, ba, ba.
Dm7/C
Ba, ba, ba,

Ba, ba, ba, ba, ba, ba.
G7
Ba, ba, ba,

Ba, ba, ba, ba, ba, ba.
Dm7/C
Ba, ba, ba,

Ba, ba, ba, ba, ba, ba.)
‖: G7 | | Dm7/C | :‖ *Repeat and fade*

Wouldn't It Be Nice

Words and Music by
Brian Wilson, Tony Asher and Mike Love

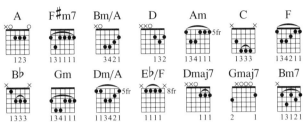

Intro | A   F♯m7 | Bm/A   D | A   F♯m7 | Am

Verse 1
        C   **F**
Would - n't it be nice if we were older,
                B♭   **Gm**
Then we wouldn't have to wait so long?
      C   **F**
And wouldn't it be nice to live together
          B♭   **Gm**   **C**
In the kind of world where we'd belong?

Chorus 1
Dm/A   **E♭/F**
  You know, it's gonna make it that much better
Dm/A   **Am**   **Gm**
  When we can say goodnight and stay togeth - er.

Verse 2
        C   **F**
  Wouldn't it be nice if we could wake up
            B♭   **Gm**
In the morning when the day is new,
      C   **F**
And after having spent the day together,
          B♭   **Gm**   **C**
Hold each other close the whole night through?

Copyright © 1966 IRVING MUSIC, INC.
Copyright Renewed
All Rights Reserved   Used by Permission

GUITAR CHORD SONGBOOK

Chorus 2

Dm/A   E♭/F
 The happy times together we've been spending,
Dm/A   Am Gm
 I wish that ev'ry kiss was neverend - ing.
C   F
 Oh, wouldn't it be __ nice?

Bridge

Dmaj7 Gmaj7
 Maybe if we think and wish

And hope and pray,
 F♯m7   Bm7
It might come true.
Dmaj7   Gmaj7
 Baby, then there wouldn't be
     F♯m7
A single thing we couldn't do.
Bm7   F♯m7
 Oh, we could be mar - ried,
Bm7   F♯m7
 And then we'd be hap - py.
C   F
 Oh, wouldn't it be __ nice?

Interlude

| F | | | | | | |

Chorus 3

Dm/A   E♭/F
 You know, it seems the more we talk about it,
Dm/A   Am Gm
 It only makes it worse to live without ___ it.
   Am Gm
But let's talk about ___ it.
C   F
 Oh, wouldn't it be __ nice?

| F | | | | |

Outro

  F
‖: Good night, oh, oh, baby.

 Sleep tight, oh, oh, baby. :‖ ***Repeat and fade***

You Still Believe in Me

Words and Music by
Brian Wilson and Tony Asher

Melody:

I know per-fect-ly well

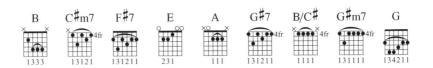

B	C#m7	F#7	E	A	G#7	B/C#	G#m7	G

Intro

| N.C.(B) | | | | |

Verse 1

    B   C#m7 F#7 B
I know perfect-ly well

        C#m7   F#7   B C#m7 F#7
I'm not where I ____should be.

   B   C#m7 F#7   B
I've been very _____ away;

           C#m7 F#7   B C#m7 F#7
You've been patient ____with me.

 E   B   A   E
Ev'ry time we ____ break up

     B   A   G#7
You bring back ____ your love to me.

        C#m7
And after all I've done to you

How can it be,

     B/C#   C#m7 G#m7 G
You still be - lieve   in   me?

Copyright © 1966 IRVING MUSIC, INC.
Copyright Renewed
All Rights Reserved   Used by Permission

Verse 2

```
          B   C#m7   F#7    B
I try hard to ___ be more
```

```
              C#m7    F#7    B    C#m7   F#7
What you want me ___ to be.
```

```
          B   C#m7    F#7    B
But I can't help how ___ I  act
```

```
              C#m7    F#7    B    C#m7   F#7
When you're not here ___ with me.
```

```
E   B     A     E
I try hard to ___ be strong,
```

```
          B          A    G#7
But sometimes ___ I fail myself.
```

```
          C#m7
And after all I've promised you so faithfully,
```

```
          B/C#    A/B   G#m7  G
You still be - lieve   in      me.
```

Interlude

```
              B   C#m7   F#7   B   C#m7   F#7
I wanna cry.
```

```
| B         C#m7  F#7  | B          C#m7  F#7  |
```

Outro

```
‖: B        C#m7  F#7  | B          C#m7  F#7 :‖  Repeat and fade
   Ah.
```

You're So Good to Me

Words and Music by
Brian Wilson and Mike Love

Melody:

You're — kind - a small

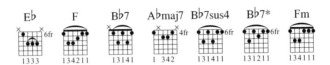

Eb	F	Bb7	Abmaj7	Bb7sus4	Bb7*	Fm

Verse 1

              Eb
You're ___ kinda small and you're such a doll,

            F
I'm glad ___ you're mine.

               Bb7
You're so good ____ to me.

              Eb
How come you ___ are?

Verse 2

           Eb
You ___ take my hand and you understand

            F
When I ___ get in a bad mood.

              Bb7
You're so good ___ to me.

Eb   **Abmaj7**
  And I love it,

Bb7sus4 **Bb7**
Love   it.

Copyright © 1965 IRVING MUSIC, INC.
Copyright Renewed
All Rights Reserved   Used by Permission

Chorus 1

E♭
La, la, la, la, la, la, la, la.

La, la, la, la, la, la, la, la.
Fm
La, la, la, la, la, la, la, la.

La, la, la, la, la, la, la, la.
E♭
La, la, la, la, la, la, la, la.

La, la, la, la, la, la, la, la.
B♭7sus4
La, la, la, la, la, la, la, la.
B♭7
La, la, la, la, la, la, la, la.

Verse 3

    E♭
I __ know your eyes are not on the guys

      F
When we're __ apart.

       B♭7
You're so true ____ to me.

       E♭
How come you __ are?

And ev'ry night you hold me so tight

     F
When I __ kiss you goodbye.

      B♭7
You're so good ____ to me.

Chorus 2   *Repeat Chorus 1*

Outro   *Repeat Chorus 1 and fade*

Wild Honey

Words and Music by
Brian Wilson and Mike Love

Melody:

Sweet, sweet   hon - ey   bee.

Intro | G | C/G | G | C/G |

G   C/G
Sweet, sweet honey bee.

G   C/G
Eat, eat a bit of honey.

Verse 1

G   C/G
Mama, I'm telling you,

                   G   C/G
As sure as I'm standing here,

              G
She's my __ girl.

        C/G
And that's the way I'm keeping it,

        G   C/G
My mama dear.

          Am
No good will it do you

        C
To stand there and frown at me.

          Am
The girl's got my heart

            C
And my love's coming down on me.

          Am
My love's coming down

            D7   G
Since I   got a taste of wild honey.

Copyright © 1967 IRVING MUSIC, INC.
Copyright Renewed
All Rights Reserved   Used by Permission